THE KENNEDYS

BY ALEXIS BURLING

CONTENT CONSULTANT
NANCY BECK YOUNG
DEPARTMENT CHAIR AND PROFESSOR
DEPARTMENT OF HISTORY, UNIVERSITY OF HOUSTON

Essential Library

An Imprint of Abdo Publishing | abdopublishing.com

abdopublishing.com

Published by Abdo Publishing, a division of ABDO, PO Box 398166, Minneapolis, Minnesota 55439. Copyright © 2016 by Abdo Consulting Group, Inc. International copyrights reserved in all countries. No part of this book may be reproduced in any form without written permission from the publisher. Essential Library™ is a trademark and logo of Abdo Publishing.

Printed in the United States of America, North Mankato, Minnesota
102015
012016

THIS BOOK CONTAINS
RECYCLED MATERIALS

Cover Photo: Corbis
Interior Photos: AP Images, 5, 8, 17, 27, 28, 35, 37, 45, 51, 56, 59, 61, 69, 73, 83, 86, 93; Red Line Editorial, 12–13; Underwood & Underwood/John F. Kennedy Presidential Library and Museum, Boston, 15; Everett Collection/Newscom, 19; John Rous/AP Images, 22; Charles Gorry/AP Images, 25; CWO Donald Mingfield/US Army Signal Corps/John F. Kennedy Presidential Library and Museum, Boston, 47; Department of Defense/AP Images, 55; Lyndon Baines Johnson Library/Newscom, 63; Ike Altgens/AP Images, 67; Bettmann/Corbis, 71, 81; Richard J. Sroda/AP Images, 75; akg-images/Newscom, 76; Ron Edmonds/AP Images, 91; Phil McCarten/Invision for the Television Academy/AP Images, 97; CSU Archives/Everett Collection, 101

Editor: Mirella Miller
Series Designer: Becky Daum

Library of Congress Control Number: 2015945393
Cataloging-in-Publication Data

Burling, Alexis.
 The Kennedys / Alexis Burling.
   p. cm. -- (America's great political families)
Includes bibliographical references and index.
ISBN 978-1-62403-909-6
1. Kennedy, John F. (John Fitzgerald), 1917-1963--Juvenile literature. 2. Kennedy family--Juvenile literature. 3. Presidents--Family relationships--United States--Biography--Juvenile literature. 4. United States--Politics and government--Juvenile literature. I. Title.
973.922/092--dc23
[B]   2015945393

CONTENTS

CHAPTER 1

ELECTION NIGHT
1960

It was the evening of Tuesday, November 8, 1960, and tension levels were running high. Men, women, and children all across the United States were camped out in their living rooms, eyes and ears glued to their television sets and radios, waiting for the voting results to roll in. Two men—47-year-old Republican Vice President Richard M. Nixon and the 43-year-old Democratic senator from Massachusetts, John F. "Jack" Kennedy—were in a hotly contested race to see who would become the next president of the United States.

At NBC News headquarters in New York City, New York, anchormen Chet Huntley and David Brinkley, both dressed in pressed suits and ties, were standing by to update the millions of viewers who had tuned

Jack, *left*, and Nixon, *right*, were both popular candidates, making the 1960 presidential election a close race.

in to election night coverage. Inside the Kennedy family compound in Hyannis Port, Massachusetts, Jack; his pregnant wife, Jacqueline "Jackie," who would give birth to their son John Jr. just two weeks later; younger brother and campaign manager, Robert "Bobby;" and a sprinkling of other campaign staff waited nervously for the returns. As the hour grew later and later into the night, it was anybody's guess

A NEW AGE OF COMPUTERS

Election night in 1960 was exciting for many reasons. It was a close race, with an incumbent Republican vice president fighting for the presidency against a relatively unseasoned Democratic senator. But outside the candidates' arena, there was an equally thrilling invention capturing viewers' attention: the computer.

Since 1952, when CBS used a computer for the first time in history to forecast Dwight D. Eisenhower's presidential win, news outlets had begun relying on machines to tally votes and offer projections of who the winner might

be. The process then was nowhere near as seamless as it is today. As soon as the totals were gathered, they were sent to an RCA 501 computer, punched out on strips of magnetic tape, fed into banks of tape storage reels, and compared to totals in past elections. This allowed reporters to predict possible election outcomes.

During the late 1950s and early 1960s, an entire RCA 501 computer system could be bought for $25,000 to $30,000. That is twice what a house in the United States cost at the time![2]

which candidate would come out on top. "These will be the longest hours of my life," said Jackie.[1]

On the Campaign Trail

Ever since the death of his older brother Joseph Jr. in 1944—a young man Joseph Sr., the family patriarch, had hoped would someday become president of the United States—Jack Kennedy's mind was fixated on a career in politics. During the previous 15 years, he had served three terms in the House of Representatives and two in the Senate. Still, fueled by his own ambitions and the expectations of Joe Sr. that one of his sons would inhabit the Oval Office, Jack had a hunch he was destined for more. In short, he wanted the presidency.

In the months since he had declared his presidential bid in January 1960 and picked Texas Senator Lyndon B. Johnson as his running mate at the Democratic convention in July, Jack had crisscrossed the country dozens of times. He had given hundreds of speeches and attended lunches and dinners to promote his Democratic agenda. He promised to fight for equal civil rights for all and to take a stand against the spread of Communism. And though Americans had never before elected a Catholic president, Jack assured the public his Catholic faith would not interfere in government affairs, nor would he allow the pope, the National Council of Churches, or any other religious organization to influence or dictate his political decisions.

By late August, a poll reported Jack's and Vice President Nixon's approval ratings were neck and neck. Jack gave his last campaign speech on November 7 in Providence, Rhode Island, to a packed auditorium full of ardent supporters. And on the morning of Election Day, he and Jackie cast their votes in the basement of a public library in Boston, Massachusetts. They then returned home to Hyannis Port for a photo session with the media on the lawn with their almost three-year-old daughter, Caroline, and a Welsh terrier named Charlie.

After months of tiring travel, 20-hour workdays, and near-constant clamoring for votes, Jack was exhausted. He tried to take a nap in advance of the evening's festivities, but did not get much sleep. In a few short hours, the world would find out whether a Kennedy would be elected to the highest office in the nation.

The Returns Roll In

At 11:00 p.m., the results from polling districts in major liberal-leaning East Coast cities started trickling in. New York City. Philadelphia and

"I believe in an America where the separation of church and state is absolute; where no Catholic prelate would tell the President—should he be Catholic—how to act, and no Protestant minister would tell his parishioners for whom to vote."[3]

—*Senator John F. Kennedy, in a speech before the Greater-Houston Ministerial Association in September 1960*

Jack makes his way through a crowd of supporters in Los Angeles, California.

Pittsburgh, Pennsylvania. Boston, Massachusetts. Hartford, Connecticut. All projected a Kennedy win. By midnight, when it became clear Chicago, Illinois, had joined its eastern counterparts in the Democratic camp, Jack's popular vote margin grew so large—2,000,000 votes—that many news outlets, including the *New York Times*, started preparing "John F. Kennedy elected!" headline copy.[4]

But as night turned into morning on November 9 and the ballots from western cities and rural areas were counted, the outcome of the election became less certain. By 5:00 a.m., Jack's lead had shrunk to 800,000 votes and the Republicans were gaining more votes by the minute. Swing states such as Washington, Hawaii, and Alaska flipped from Republican to Democrat and back again. If Jack was going to win, he would need to win one of three undecided states—California, Minnesota, or Illinois—to secure the 269 electoral votes required for the presidency.[5]

Finally, at 12:33 p.m., NBC made a historic announcement. The votes had been counted: Jack had gained Minnesota and secured the presidency. With 303 electoral votes to Vice President Nixon's 219, and 34,226,731 popular votes to Nixon's 34,108,157, it was one of the closest elections in US history.[6] At 12:46 p.m., Nixon made his concession speech.

Jack and the rest of his family and campaign staff were elated. Not only was he the youngest man to win the presidency, but he was also the nation's first Catholic to do so. After years of living in Joe Jr.'s shadow and wondering whether he could achieve success on his own, Jack had accomplished what his father had always dreamed of—a Kennedy in the White House. In two months, Jack would become the thirty-fifth president of the United States.

A TRUTHFUL VICTORY?

Though Jack was declared the victor on November 9, 1960, many Republicans contended the senator did not win fair and square. Rumors circulated that voter fraud had occurred in potentially 11 states. In Chicago, Mayor Richard Daly—a Kennedy supporter—supposedly allowed the votes of dead people to pass as legitimate. In some counties throughout Texas—Jack's running mate Lyndon Johnson's home state—there were more votes counted than actual registered voters in the district.

Recounts were held in hundreds of precincts and counties across the United States, and in some cases, such as in Chicago, the courts and the Federal Bureau of Investigation got involved. In the end, most of the court cases were dismissed or the recount discrepancies were not significant enough to alter the outcome of the election. Nixon declined to contest the results, and Jack was sworn into office on January 20, 1961. While most historians agree the election was far from clean, the legitimacy of Jack's presidential win is no longer questioned.

KENNEDY FAMILY TREE

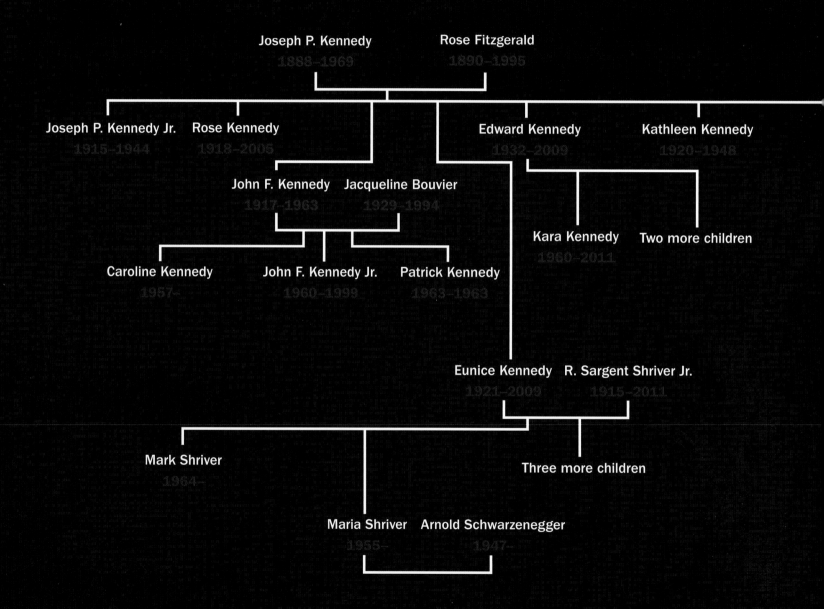

Joseph P. Kennedy
1888–1969

Rose Fitzgerald
1890–1995

Joseph P. Kennedy Jr.
1915–1944

Rose Kennedy
1918–2005

Edward Kennedy
1932–2009

Kathleen Kennedy
1920–1948

John F. Kennedy
1917–1963

Jacqueline Bouvier
1929–1994

Kara Kennedy
1960–2011

Two more children

Caroline Kennedy
1957–

John F. Kennedy Jr.
1960–1999

Patrick Kennedy
1963–1963

Eunice Kennedy
1921–2009

R. Sargent Shriver Jr.
1915–2011

Mark Shriver
1964–

Three more children

Maria Shriver
1955–

Arnold Schwarzenegger
1947–

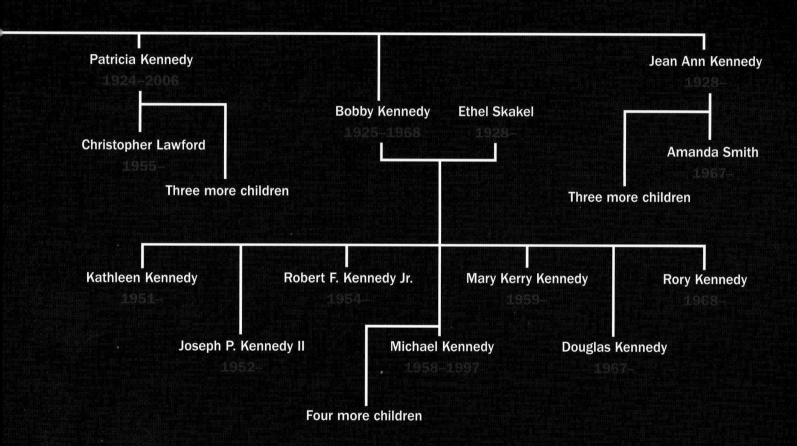

Patricia Kennedy
1924–2006

Christopher Lawford
1955–

Three more children

Bobby Kennedy
1925–1968

Ethel Skakel
1928–

Jean Ann Kennedy
1928–

Amanda Smith
1967–

Three more children

Kathleen Kennedy
1951–

Robert F. Kennedy Jr.
1954–

Mary Kerry Kennedy
1959–

Rory Kennedy
1968–

Joseph P. Kennedy II
1952–

Michael Kennedy
1958–1997

Douglas Kennedy
1967–

Four more children

13

CHAPTER 2

THE PATRIARCH

For more than a century, the Kennedy family has played a crucial role in politics. From matters of civil rights and international diplomacy to policies affecting education and economic reform, nearly eight generations of Kennedys have had a hand in shaping the way the US government and social systems run. While he would never have the chance to realize his own lofty ambitions during his lifetime, the man most responsible for setting his children on a path to political greatness was the family patriarch, Joseph P. Kennedy.

Joe was born in Boston on September 6, 1888, to Irish Catholic parents, socialite Mary Hickey and Patrick Joseph Kennedy. Joe's father, often called "PJ," was a leader in local politics. He served in both the

Joe was an ambitious businessman in the early 1930s.

> **"You must remember, it's not what you are that counts, but what people think you are."[1]**
> *—As Joseph P. Kennedy often told his children*

Massachusetts House of Representatives and Senate and, in a stint that lasted for more than 30 years, as the head of East Boston's Ward 2, where he chaired committees and gathered votes during elections. PJ also dabbled in liquor sales and finance. By the time Joe graduated from the prestigious Boston Latin School—the oldest public school in the United States—in 1908, PJ had a hand in setting up both the Columbia Trust Company and the Sumner Savings Bank.

Because Joe showed an early interest in business and governmental affairs, it seemed as though he was destined to follow in his father's footsteps. He was accepted at Harvard University, where he played football, baseball, and basketball. He was also the captain of the tennis team. But something else was also occupying Joe's attention during his time at Harvard—or, more accurately, someone. Her name was Rose Fitzgerald.

The Apple of Joe's Eye

From the moment he had laid eyes on Rose Fitzgerald in Old Orchard Beach, Maine, a popular vacation spot for many of Boston's Irish Catholics, Joe knew she was the girl for him. Rose was the eldest daughter of Josie Hannon and John Francis

Fitzgerald, a politician who served one term in the Massachusetts State Senate, two terms in the US House of Representatives, and two nonconsecutive terms as mayor of Boston. Known as "Honey Fitz" in political circles, Rose's father was one of the most well-connected men in Boston. He was "loud, brash, unrestrained on the stump, an indefatigable backslapper and hand-shaker."[2] Though he adored his daughter, he was not fond of Joe and did everything in his power to keep them apart, especially after Rose and Joe became an official couple when they were both in their late teens.

But Joe and Rose refused to let Honey Fitz's meddling get in the way of their dreams. "There's no question that young Joe Kennedy saw Rose as the catch of Boston, maybe even of America at that time," says historian Doris Kearns Goodwin.[3] While attending classes at Manhattanville College, starting an elite social club for prominent Irish Catholic

Rose grew up in a wealthy politician's family in Boston.

HONEY FITZ INTERFERES

Joe and Rose enjoyed a long courtship. None of their parents approved, especially Rose's father. Honey Fitz forbade Rose to attend high school functions with Joe, but with the help of friends and the Fitzgeralds' chauffeur, the two lovebirds managed to meet in secret. "It took teamwork and conspiracy, because we needed reliable allies," said Rose.[4]

Soon Honey Fitz took more drastic measures to keep his daughter and Joe apart. In 1908, he whisked 18-year-old Rose and her sister Agnes away to Europe for vacation and enrolled them in a Sacred Heart convent near Belgium for a year of schooling. When 23-year-old Joe invited Rose to Harvard's junior prom in 1911, Honey Fitz sent her to Palm Beach, Florida, and then to Europe again for six weeks, followed by Central and South America. Nothing her father did could keep Rose and Joe from pursuing each other. When she announced their intention to marry in 1914, Honey Fitz finally agreed to their wishes.

young ladies called the Lenox Avenue Club, and planning her debutante party, Rose continued to date Joe against her father's wishes. Finally, on October 7, 1914—two years after Joe graduated from Harvard—the pair got married.

Joe and Rose's wedding was, by high society's standards, an intimate gathering. The reception, with 75 guests on the invitation list, took place at the Fitzgeralds' home in Dorchester, a neighborhood of Boston. For their honeymoon, the newlyweds spent a couple of weeks touring the Northeast, with stops in New York; Atlantic City in New Jersey; Philadelphia, where they saw the 1914 World Series; and a chic resort in White Sulphur Springs, West Virginia. On their return home, they moved to a quaint wood-framed house in the Boston suburb of Brookline, at 83 Beals Street.

A Full House Divided

The first decade of Joe and Rose's marriage was a whirlwind of activity, mostly because of their ever-expanding family. The couple had five children in six years—Joe Jr., Jack, Rosemary, Kathleen "Kick," and Eunice. Three more soon followed—Patricia, Bobby, and Jean Ann. By the time the last Kennedy— Edward "Ted"—was born on February 22, 1932, Joe and Rose had practically built a dynasty.

"I think that when we stood as a blushing, radiant, gay young bride and groom, we were not able to look ahead and see nine little helpless infants with our responsibility to turn them into men and women who were mentally, morally and physically perfect,"

Joe and Rose pose after their wedding ceremony in 1914.

THE KENNEDY CARD CATALOG

With nine children in the house, Rose had quite a time keeping track of their comings and goings. She had a staff full of cooks, maids, drivers, and governesses to watch over their affairs. How did she ensure her kids' daily needs were being met? First she installed a bulletin board where she would post notes, reminders, and topics of discussion for mealtime conversation. Then she created a card catalog where she would write down their developmental milestones. Doctor's appointments, illnesses, immunizations, successes at school—all of this information was dutifully recorded. Having nine children was certainly a handful, but Rose's supreme organizational skills assured the house was in orderly shape at all times.

Rose wrote later.[5] But with the help of a full-time staff of nannies, chauffeurs, and maids—and thanks to Rose's superb organizational skills and diligence—the Kennedy family flourished.

While Rose busied herself with managing the household, Joe Sr. concentrated exclusively on his career, working long hours at the office and taking separate vacations from his wife. At 25 years old, he took over the bank his father had started, Columbia Trust, and became the youngest bank president in the country. Beginning in 1917, when he turned 29, he moved through a series of jobs, including becoming an assistant general manager at the Fore River Shipbuilding Corporation's plant in Quincy, Massachusetts, where he met future president Franklin Delano Roosevelt, who was assistant secretary of the navy at that time. Joe Sr. also became a familiar face on

Wall Street, first as a stockbroker at Hayden, Stone, and Company, and then as an independent banker in 1923. By the time three years had passed, he had amassed more than $2 million—a substantial fortune.[6]

Winds of Change

With his success on Wall Street, Joe Sr. decided it was time for a change—both at home and in his career. In 1927, the 39-year-old moved his family to a lavish two-year rental in the Bronx, and then to a permanent mansion in Bronxville, New York, 15 miles (24 km) from midtown Manhattan. He purchased another vacation home in Palm Beach, Florida. And never wanting to be too far from their Massachusetts roots, the Kennedys began spending their summers on a sprawling estate in Hyannis Port on Cape Cod, approximately one hour outside Boston.

With Rose fully occupied by her duties as Kennedy matriarch, Joe Sr. expanded his employment prospects outward and upward. He journeyed to Hollywood, California, for months at a time and spent three years running a film studio, creating low-budget action flicks and having extramarital affairs with starlets. After his stint as a movie producer ended in 1931, Joe Sr. threw all of his focus onto politics by linking himself to an old colleague who was running for president on the Democratic ticket: Franklin D. Roosevelt.

When Roosevelt was elected president in November 1932, Joe assumed he would be offered the secretary of the treasury position because of his experience on Wall Street. But he was passed over twice. Instead, Roosevelt appointed Joe to two non-cabinet positions. From 1934 to 1935, Joe served as chairman of the Securities and Exchange Commission, a fledgling organization in charge of regulating the manipulation of stock prices. Then, after publishing a book called *I'm for Roosevelt*,

The Kennedy compound in Hyannis Port, Massachusetts, continues to be a vacation destination for Kennedy family members.

A HOLLYWOOD AFFAIR

When Joe ventured to Hollywood to make films, the movie industry was in transition. Silent films, movies without dialogue, were still popular, but they were slowly being replaced by "talkies," which included speaking actors and music. Joe enjoyed creating low-budget, commercial movies for theaters, from Westerns to stunt thrillers. He also had extramarital affairs with beautiful actresses. His favorite was Gloria Swanson, a brunette bombshell with whom he coproduced a number of films, including the flop *Queen Kelly*.

Though Joe and Swanson's affair lasted for years, Rose turned a blind eye because, as a devout Catholic, divorce was not an option. "I have no doubt Rose knew what was going on. But in my judgment, she willed that knowledge out of her mind," says historian Doris Kearns Goodwin. "She didn't want to lose her marriage. She didn't want to lose her husband. She didn't want to lose that family she had created—it mattered too much to her."[7]

written to convince business owners to get behind Roosevelt's reelection, Joe was named head of the newly established US Maritime Commission in 1936, during Roosevelt's second term. It would be Joe's job to revitalize the United States' merchant shipping industry.

As 1937 wound down, however, Joe was confident he was destined for more political responsibility. He even had his eyes on the presidential nomination as the next Democratic candidate when Roosevelt's second term concluded. But Roosevelt had other ideas. Believing Joe to be untrustworthy, Roosevelt wanted Joe out of

CRITICS APPROVE

When Joe was appointed chairman of the Securities and Exchange Commission, many people were appalled by Roosevelt's choice for the job. Joe had amassed most of his fortune through risky investments in the stock market. His critics were sure he would use those same tactics on the job. But they were wrong; Joe reformed Wall Street by outlawing the shady practices he had adopted in the past. And when he left the position, his former naysayers were pleased with his success. "Kennedy has done one of the best jobs of anyone connected with the New Deal," wrote a reporter from the *Washington Post*.[8]

the country altogether and removed him from the sphere of influence. In December 1937, he appointed Joe ambassador to the Court of Saint James in the United Kingdom. The following year, the Kennedys—all 11 of them—would begin a new life overseas in London, England.

Joe, *left,* is sworn in as ambassador to the Court of Saint James in front of President Roosevelt, *sitting*, and Associate Justice Stanley F. Reed, *center.*

CHAPTER 3

THE KENNEDYS AT WAR

For the Kennedys in 1938, life in England was different than anything they had known in the past. Unlike in Hyannis Port or Palm Beach, where they were often snubbed because of their Irish Catholic roots, in London they were treated like dignitaries. They moved into a six-story, 52-room mansion with manicured grounds and an elevator. Except for Joe Jr. and Jack, who both attended Harvard and came to visit during summer breaks, all the Kennedy children were enrolled at various British schools.

Once again, Rose took control as mother and social coordinator extraordinaire, supporting her husband's efforts behind the scenes. She attended balls, luncheons, and fancy teas and socialized with high society's crowd, including the king and queen at Windsor Castle.

Joe, Rose, *left of Joe*, and some of their children walk through London after Joe's appointment as ambassador.

She also threw lavish parties, such as the debutante celebrations for her oldest daughters, Rosemary and Kick.

Joe's time in London was busy spent meeting with other diplomats and Prime Minister Neville Chamberlain.

Joe kept busy forging business relationships and strengthening ties with members of the British Parliament. He attended countless government meetings, reporting his findings to President Roosevelt. He also tried to gain approval from British Prime Minister Neville Chamberlain. This proved especially tricky as the threat of a second world war loomed and Joe's opinion that the United States should stay out of the war was in direct contrast with that of British leaders and of President Roosevelt.

When German Chancellor Adolf Hitler invaded Poland on September 1, 1939, and the United Kingdom prepared to declare war against Germany, Joe's insistent recommendation for appeasement triggered his downfall. "Try as he might, he could not quite do what was expected of him," wrote biographer David Nasaw. "[Joe] was simply unfitted by temperament for the position of impartial, impassive listener and reporter, especially at moments of crisis."[1] The British government tapped Joe's phone lines, and he was ridiculed in the press and called a coward for not supporting the war effort. Finally, in October 1940, one year after he sent his family back to Hyannis Port, Joe returned to the United States, defeated.

The Kennedy Kids Do Their Part

In November 1940, 52-year-old Joe submitted his formal resignation as US ambassador to the United Kingdom. With his political career in shambles, he began the process of transferring his presidential aspirations to his sons, Joe Jr. and Jack. After graduating from

"DEMOCRACY IS FINISHED!"

In 1940, President Roosevelt was elected to an unprecedented third term as president to take the United States through World War II (1939–1945). Though Joe once again participated in his reelection campaign, Roosevelt refused to keep him on staff. He found Joe's pacifist approach to the war distasteful, especially because it made him appear easygoing on Hitler's extermination of the Jewish people. After an off-the-record interview with a reporter from the *Boston Sunday Globe* on November 10, 1940, in which Joe was quoted saying, "Democracy is finished in England. It may be here [too]," Roosevelt asked for Joe's resignation from his post as US diplomat to the United Kingdom.[2] Joe's political career was over.

Harvard with honors, Joe Jr. worked briefly as his father's secretary while in England. If all went according to plan, he would be the next Kennedy in line to run for office.

Rather than jump directly into the political realm, the elder Kennedy children set their sights on aiding the war effort. Kick volunteered for the Red Cross in New York throughout 1940, raising money for the Allied Relief Fund. She then worked briefly

ROSEMARY KENNEDY

Rosemary was the third child of Rose and Joe Sr. Rosemary never made it past elementary school because of a learning disability. When she returned home from London in 1940, the 22-year-old started suffering from seizures. "She was becoming increasingly irritable and difficult," her younger sister, Eunice, wrote later.[3]

Joe Sr. decided to fix the problem without consulting his wife. He scheduled Rosemary for a prefrontal lobotomy—an experimental procedure that would sever the neural connections between the brain's prefrontal lobes to relieve the symptoms his daughter was experiencing. The surgery was unsuccessful, leaving Rosemary with permanent brain damage and unable to speak. In 1948, Joe Sr. installed her in a nursing home in Jefferson, Wisconsin, where she would stay until her death on January 7, 2005, at age 86.

Rose never forgave her husband for what happened to Rosemary. In 1962, Eunice created an organization in Rosemary's honor. Eunice started a summer camp in her backyard for people with intellectual disabilities. The camp led to the creation of the Special Olympics, a global competition attracting 4.4 million athletes from 170 countries.[4]

for the *Washington Times-Herald* as a reviewer and society reporter before heading back to London to work for the Red Cross in 1943. It was there the 23-year-old met and fell in love with the handsome and wealthy William Cavendish Hartington, widely considered to be "the most eligible bachelor in England."[5] The two married on May 6, 1944, despite Rose's disapproval of Hartington's Protestant faith. Sadly, Kick became a widow four months later when her husband was killed in combat on September 10.

Meanwhile, after graduating from Harvard, both Joe Jr. and Jack enlisted in the military. In 1941, Jack entered training for the navy in the Office of Naval Intelligence. Due to frequent illnesses as a child that left his body in poor shape—including a near-fatal bout of scarlet fever when he was nearly three—Jack was given a desk job rather than active duty. But after the Japanese bombed Pearl Harbor, Hawaii, on December 7, 1941, triggering the United States' official entry into the war, he was sent to the South Pacific as the lieutenant in charge of a patrol torpedo boat, *PT-109*.

Jack's time in the navy was short-lived. A Japanese destroyer rammed into the side of *PT-109*, slicing it in half on August 2, 1943. Two of the boat's crew died when the battered ship burst into flames. Though Jack and the rest of his men were rescued after spending hours in the frigid ocean and six days on a deserted island, an injury to Jack's back would prevent him from continuing to serve. After his return home, Jack was awarded the Navy and Marine Corps Medal for his courage in bringing his men to safety.

A MESSAGE SCRATCHED INTO A COCONUT

When a Japanese destroyer ripped his boat apart, Jack was instrumental in shepherding ten members of his crew to freedom. Despite his injured back, he carried one of the men onto the shore of a barren island by clenching one of the lifejacket straps between his teeth and tugging the man along as he swam. Jack carved an SOS message into a coconut shell. When Eroni Kumana and Biuku Gasa, residents of a neighboring island, discovered the stranded navy men a few days later, Jack handed them the shell. Kumana and Gasa paddled 35 miles (56 km) to deliver its message to the nearest Allied base. The next morning—six days after the *PT-109* crew had arrived on the island—Jack and his crew were rescued.

Heartbreak

Despite Jack's ongoing health concerns and the constant threat of war breaking out on US soil, nothing could prepare the Kennedys for the unexpected tragedy that would soon befall their family. Joe Jr. had become a pilot in 1942 and was sent to England with the first naval squadron to fly B-24 airplanes for the British Naval Command. He had flown many missions and watched many of his friends die. After two years, he completed his tour of duty and was due to be sent home in May 1944.

But 29-year-old Joe Jr. refused to leave. Instead, he continued to fly one dangerous assignment after another. And on August 12, 1944, he volunteered for the riskiest mission of all. He was tasked with flying a bomber plane packed with 21,170 pounds (9,600 kg) of explosives toward an enemy rocket-launching site in Normandy, France. Joe Jr. and his copilot were supposed to bail out so as not to get hurt, abandoning the bomber to crash into the target. But the plan went horribly wrong. The plane unexpectedly exploded before Joe Jr. and his copilot had a chance to eject themselves. They were both killed instantly.

Upon hearing the news, the Kennedy family gathered in Hyannis Port and went into a period of deep mourning. Even Joe Sr., usually so focused on work, took months off to honor Joe Jr.'s death. Nearly two years passed. By 1946, Joe Sr. felt it was time to get back in the game. If Joe Sr. had anything to do with it, Jack would take his older brother's place and establish a Kennedy foothold in politics.

"It may be felt, perhaps, that Joe should not have pushed his luck so far and should have accepted his leave and come home. But two facts must be borne in mind. First, at the time of his death, he had completed probably more combat missions in heavy bombers than any other pilot of his rank in the Navy and therefore was preeminently qualified, and secondly, as he told a friend early in August, he considered the odds at least fifty-fifty, and Joe never asked for any better odds than that."[6]

—Jack Kennedy, following Joe Jr.'s death

CHAPTER 4

A BID FOR THE PRESIDENCY

It was the fall of 1945, and World War II had finally ended. The Allies, led by the United States, the United Kingdom, the Soviet Union, China, and France, had defeated the Axis powers—Germany, Italy, and Japan. The United States was in transition on the home front as well. After Roosevelt's sudden death from a cerebral hemorrhage on April 12, Vice President Harry S. Truman became the United States' thirty-third president.

According to Joe Sr., there was no better time for jump-starting Jack's career in politics. But before running for Massachusetts's eleventh congressional district seat—the same one his grandfather held 50 years earlier—the once careless and rebellious 29-year-old needed a thorough

Jack had a lot of work ahead of him in order to win his congressional campaign.

makeover. "This pasty-looking faced kid, he didn't look any more like a Boston politician that was going to go to Congress than the man in the moon, to be perfectly truthful," remembers Thomas P. O'Neill Jr., the former Democratic speaker of the House of Representatives.[1]

Rose and Honey Fitz schooled Jack in the basics of local politics and delivered lessons on how to be a trustworthy candidate who could appeal to both rich and working-class voters. These were tips Jack would use throughout his career. Joe Sr. took charge of Jack's public relations campaign. Biographer Doris Kearns Goodwin says of Joe Sr. on Jack's campaign:

> *Joe understood that whatever Jack's qualities . . . were, that he had to be marketed. And I suppose he thought he had to be marketed the way any stock was marketed, the way anything in business was marketed. He used that to make sure that the people understood he was a war hero, even more of a war hero than he actually was, and that he had these kinds of family qualities that people were going to want to see in their politicians.[2]*

In 1946, Jack was elected to Congress in a landslide against Republican Lester Brown and Prohibitionist Philip Geer, with 69,093 votes.[3] At first, he appeared naïve and inexperienced as he debated and voted on issues concerning the economy, affordable housing for war veterans, and foreign policy. But despite being diagnosed

Jack, his parents, and several supporters celebrate his win in 1946.

with Addison's disease—a potentially fatal disease of the adrenal glands that causes circulation failure—one year into his first term and enduring near-constant debilitating back pain as a result, Jack continued to serve two more terms in the House of Representatives.

THE KENNEDYS SUFFER ANOTHER LOSS

After the death of her first husband, Kick journeyed back to the United States briefly before returning to England to settle permanently. She still mourned the loss of her first husband, Lord Hartington, but had begun courting the attention of an unhappily married man, Earl Peter Wentworth-Fitzwilliam, in 1946. On May 13, 1948, 28-year-old Kick and Fitzwilliam were on their way to a vacation in France when their plane experienced turbulence and crashed into the French Alps. Both died instantly.

Jack's Years in the Senate

By 1952, carrying six years of political experience under his belt, Jack was ready for a change. With his family once again behind him, he started campaigning for the US Senate. His 26-year-old younger brother, Bobby, who had just graduated from the University of Virginia Law School, was his campaign manager. Joe Sr. helped Jack get acclimated to using television, creating ads explaining Jack's political agenda. The Kennedy women did their part, too. With Jack's cousin Pauline in the lead, they hosted "meet-the-candidate" teas across the state to pick up more votes.

When the final numbers were tallied, Jack beat the Republican incumbent Henry Cabot Lodge Jr. by 70,000 votes, despite an overwhelming win for Republicans in the national elections.[4] It was true what Jack's Senate campaign song said: "Who can

THE KENNEDY TEAS

Bobby and Joe Sr. were instrumental in getting Jack elected to the Senate. Perhaps the most surprising bump in votes can be attributed to the Kennedy women. Led by cousin Polly Fitzgerald, with the help of Rose and her daughters, a series of teas were held in homes and hotel banquet halls across Massachusetts to introduce women to Jack's ideas.

The first tea was held at the Bancroft Hotel in Worcester. One thousand women were invited; 5,000 showed up. Dressed in expensive attire, the attendees were so thrilled with the experience and Jack's charm that support for Jack spread like wildfire across the state. "Polly and her team of assistants created a brilliant grass-roots organization," Senator Ted Kennedy later wrote. "They had 33 teas in all . . . and the excitement and enthusiasm they generated helped carry the day for Jack."[6]

fight and fight till he wins? / Kennedy can, Kennedy can / Who can do the job he begins? / Kennedy can, Kennedy can!"[5]

Jack's two terms in the Senate were filled with ups and downs, both in and out of Congress. He started courting a whip-smart, highly fashionable photographer from the *Washington Times-Herald* named Jackie Bouvier, who had studied at the prestigious Sorbonne school in Paris, France, and had just broken off an engagement with a Wall Street investment banker. On September 12, 1953, Jack, who was 36 at the time, and Jackie, who was 24, were married in front of more than 600 congressmen, diplomats, and high society guests at St. Mary's Church in Newport,

Rhode Island. Nearly 2,000 other onlookers waited outside.[7] Four years later, after a miscarriage in 1955 and a stillborn child in 1956, a healthy Caroline was born on November 27, 1957.

On the political front, Jack's world was changing as well. After taking a six-month leave of absence in 1954 following a botched back surgery that nearly killed him, a development that was kept secret from the press, he took a more active role in Congress. He published a book called *Profiles in Courage* that became a best seller in 1956 and won the Pulitzer Prize the following year. He picked up a coveted seat on the Senate Foreign Relations Committee, acted as chairman of the Senate Subcommittee on Labor Reform, and helped initiate the food-for-peace program, through which the United States donated food to emerging nations. Jack also put in his name for the vice presidential nomination in 1956 to run with presidential candidate Adlai Stevenson, but lost to Estes Kefauver, the Democratic senator from Tennessee. Still, by the turn of the decade, Jack wanted more. He was ready to try for the biggest political challenge of all—a campaign for the presidency.

"A politician has to have a wife, and a Catholic politician has to have a Catholic wife. She should have class. Jackie probably has more class than any girl we've ever seen around here."[8]

—Joseph P. Kennedy

A Challenger to Vice President Nixon

On January 2, 1960, Jack officially announced his intention to run for president. For the next six months, he campaigned hard. He vowed to fix racial discrimination, especially in schools where most blacks and whites were still segregated, and endorsed the work of civil rights leader Martin Luther King Jr. He supported the separation between church and state and assured Protestant and Jewish voters the Catholic Church and other religious bodies would not be permitted to interfere on issues such as abortion and birth control. And he advocated for strengthening US military forces to combat Soviet influence and the

AN UNFAITHFUL MARRIAGE

According to many in the press, Jack and Jackie symbolized a picture-perfect couple. What was going on behind the scenes was an entirely different matter, and most everyone knew about it, including Jackie. "There was plenty of talk about Kennedy's womanizing and the talk was just universal," said George Reedy, special assistant to Vice President Johnson.[9] Throughout his presidency, Jack carried on extramarital affairs with countless women, including Judith Campbell, who attracted the Federal Bureau of Investigation's attention because of her ties to the mob; Pamela Turnure, Jackie's press secretary; Mimi Beardsley, a 19-year-old White House intern; and Marilyn Monroe, one of Hollywood's sexiest actresses, who starred in blockbuster films such as *Gentlemen Prefer Blondes* and *Some Like It Hot*.

COLD WAR POLITICS IN SPACE

Perhaps one of the biggest issues facing the presidential candidates in the 1960 election was the threat of Communism and Soviet dominance throughout the world. Referred to as the Cold War, relations between the United States and the Soviet Union were persistently strained, especially with regard to nuclear weapons and which country might be the first to use them in a new war.

The Cold War also affected space. On October 4, 1957, the Soviets used an intercontinental ballistic missile to launch the first object into Earth's orbit—a satellite called Sputnik, which means "traveler" in Russian. The maneuver set off a race between the two countries to see which could build a more impressive space program. In 1958, the US National Aeronautics and Space Administration (NASA) was created, and in a speech on September 12, 1962, Jack declared the United States would put a man on the moon by the end of the decade:

Space is there, and we're going to climb it, and the moon and the planets are there, and new hopes for knowledge and peace are there. And, therefore, as we set sail we ask God's blessing on the most hazardous and dangerous and greatest adventure on which man has ever embarked.[10]

His prediction came true. On July 20, 1969, Neil Armstrong took the first lunar step.

rising threat of Communist dominance over free-market economies and democracy around the world.

Jackie penned a syndicated weekly newspaper column called Campaign Wife and launched Calling for Kennedy, a get-out-the-vote campaign directed at female voters. Jack's brother Bobby and Joe Sr. solicited donations from supporters. Some people claim this included mob bosses with ties to a gritty underworld full of crimes and illegal activity. Even 28-year-old Ted traveled across the country and solicited votes for his brother.

Jack faced tough competition from Hubert Humphrey, the overtly liberal senator from Minnesota; former governor of Illinois Adlai E. Stevenson, who had been the Democratic nominee in 1952 and 1956; and Senate Majority Leader Lyndon B. Johnson from Texas, whose supporters were mainly from the South. Thanks in part to the far-reaching influence of Jack's campaign that lobbied hard for the 761 votes needed for the presidential nomination, Jack was selected as the Democratic nominee when the Democratic convention was held in July 1960.[11] To the surprise of many, he

PROFILES IN COURAGE CONTROVERSY

In 1956, Jack published a book containing eight short biographies of senators whose ideas and gumption he admired. "When you're talking about political courage, you mean somebody who's willing to go against the wishes of his constituents for what he considers the best interests of the country," he wrote. Not long after it was published, a controversy erupted on national television. ABC News reported that accusations had surfaced that suggested Ted Sorenson, Jack's aide, wrote the book. Jack vehemently denied the claims. Joe Sr. was so furious he sued ABC for $50 million. In the end, ABC retracted the story. "The author of Profiles in Courage was John F. Kennedy," Sorensen said in a statement. "The author is the man who stands behind what is there on the printed page. It's his responsibility to put his name to it and to put it out."[12]

asked Johnson to be his running mate. "Everyone is voting for Jack / 'Cause he's got what all the rest lack," sang supporter Frank Sinatra as the winner was announced. "Jack is on the right track / 'Cause he's got high hopes / He's got high hopes."[13]

The contest between 43-year-old Jack and current Republican Vice President Richard Nixon was brutal. Up until the end, voters were divided on who they thought would be the better president. If there was one thing that might have pushed Jack over the finish line, it was the series of four televised debates between the candidates, the first ever to be televised during a presidential election. Seventy million people tuned in to watch. Nixon, suffering from a knee injury, looked exhausted and sweaty.[14] Jack, who had started taking cortisone for his back pain, appeared healthy and approachable. Perhaps the difference in appearance contributed to Nixon's demise.

It was the closest election in nearly a century. But by its conclusion, the voters had spoken. Jack had beaten Nixon by a margin of one-tenth of one percent.[15] Joe Sr.'s dreams had finally been realized; a Kennedy would soon take control of the White House.

Jack's appearance and confidence during the debates may have helped him secure his spot as president.

CHAPTER 5

A KENNEDY IN THE WHITE HOUSE

As 43-year-old Jack stood atop the stage at the Capitol Building on January 20, 1961—the day of his presidential inauguration—it was bitterly cold in Washington. Brisk winds whisked scarves and top hats into the air as the crowd huddled together, listening to singer Marian Anderson belt out the national anthem and 87-year-old Robert Frost recite his poem "The Gift Outright." As Jack took his place behind the podium, it was as if time stood still and all the world stopped to hear the thirty-fifth president of the United States speak.

"We observe today not a victory of party but a celebration of freedom—symbolizing an end as well as a beginning—signifying renewal as well as change," Jack began.[1] In his speech, Jack spoke plainly about

Audiences were captivated by Jack's speech at his inauguration event on January 20, 1961.

> "And so, my fellow Americans: ask not what your country can do for you—ask what you can do for your country. My fellow citizens of the world: ask not what America will do for you, but what together we can do for the freedom of man."[2]
> —John F. Kennedy, inaugural address, January 20, 1961

many of the deep-seated issues facing the United States during the 1960s. These included inequality and civil rights, poverty and disease, and the ever-looming threat of a nuclear attack. He talked of forming a global alliance to fight tyranny and prevent war. And he sounded a valiant call to action not only to the people in his great nation, but to their allies around the world.

It would be a tough road ahead. But because of Jack's contagious charisma and trusted team of advisers—including his brother Bobby as attorney general—many Americans felt confident they were in good hands.

The Threat of Communism

Jack's foreign policy skills were put to the test almost as soon as he entered the Oval Office. Before the inauguration, he was informed of a covert operation concocted by the Central Intelligence Agency (CIA) and former President Eisenhower's administration. The plan called for sending a CIA-trained group of Cuban exiles into Cuba to spark an overthrow of Fidel Castro's Communist government. Cuba's was the first Communist regime in the Western Hemisphere, and the United States perceived it as a threat to democratic influence in the region. Jack gave the go-ahead to launch the invasion. But on April 17, when rebels landed in the Bay of Pigs off the coast of southern Cuba, the United States did not provide the necessary air support. As a result, Castro's 20,000 army soldiers captured nearly 1,200 men. More than 100 of the rebel troops died.[3]

JACKIE'S WHITE HOUSE ON DISPLAY

When the Kennedys moved into the White House, it was in a state of disrepair. The First Lady's toilet did not flush and her shower did not work. The furniture was shabby and uninviting. So Jackie devoted her first year in the White House to renovating each room.

After spending the $50,000 allocated for White House redecoration in two weeks, she formed the Fine Arts Committee, featuring 16 museum curators and two scholars who would locate authentic furniture from the time the White House was built and other key periods in history.[4] They would also raise money for the cause.

The results were magnificent. The Red Room contained furniture from the early 1800s Franco-American empire. The Lincoln Bedroom was redone in the Victorian style. And she made the living quarters more kid-friendly and fun for Caroline and John Jr. When the renovations were complete, Jackie, who usually preferred to stay out of the public eye, filmed a tour of the Executive Mansion for CBS Television on February 14, 1962. A record audience of 56 million viewers tuned in.[5]

JACK'S TEAM

Presidents appoint a team of advisers when they begin office. These were some of the members of Jack's team:

- Attorney General—Bobby Kennedy
- Secretary of State—Dean Rusk
- Secretary of the Treasury—C. Douglas Dillon
- Secretary of Defense—Robert S. McNamara
- National Security Adviser—McGeorge Bundy
- Secretary of Agriculture—Orville L. Freeman
- Secretary of the Interior—Stewart L. Udall
- Ambassador to the United Nations—Adlai Stevenson
- Press Secretary—Pierre Salinger

The US government's failed takeover was Jack's first embarrassment and an obvious mistake. He fired the head of the CIA and pledged to involve his brother Bobby in all matters of government moving forward, including enlisting his help in Operation Mongoose—a secret, ongoing effort to force Castro from power. But the Communism problem did not end with Cuba. On April 29, Jack approved the deploying of 500 Special Forces troops to the southern half of Vietnam, which was under siege by Communist Vietcong in the North. Over the next two years, he would increase those numbers to more than 16,000 troops.[6] Though some historians believe Jack issued an order to pull US troops out of Vietnam in October 1963, his initial military commitment to stopping the spread of

Communism across Southeast Asia had long-lasting effects through the next decade and beyond.

Then, in June 1961, Jack attended a meeting in Vienna, Austria, with Nikita Khrushchev, leader of the Soviet Union, to discuss the issues surrounding Berlin, Germany, among other matters. As part of the settlement terms after World War II, the German capital of Berlin had been divided among the winning Allies. West Berlin was under the control of the United States, the United Kingdom, and France, while the Communist Soviets occupied East Berlin. At the June summit, Khrushchev demanded that Jack withdraw US forces from West Berlin so the city could be unified under Communist control. Jack refused; instead, he sent 150,000 additional troops to the area.[7] Two months later, on August 13, Khrushchev

Jack delivers a speech on the failed mission in Cuba and its consequences, such as threats from the Soviet Union.

CHECKPOINT CHARLIE

For a tense few hours on October 27–28, 1961, an altercation on a street corner in Berlin nearly set off a third world war. Since the construction of the Berlin Wall, a series of checkpoints were set up so armed guards could verify the travel papers of anyone intending to pass between East and West Berlin. At one of the checkpoints, a dispute developed over whether US diplomats should be allowed free access between the open and closed sections of the city. On the morning of October 27, Berliners awoke to find US and Soviet tanks stationed on either side of the wall. It was a 16-hour standoff.

Luckily, Jack prevented further escalation via back-channel negotiations with the Soviet government. Khrushchev backed down, and Jack followed suit. Though the Berlin Wall stayed in place until 1989, Soviet and Western diplomats and military personnel were allowed unrestricted access to life on either side.

retaliated by erecting the Berlin Wall—a cinderblock and barbed wire barrier 12 feet (3.7 m) tall and 4 feet (1.2 m) wide separating East and West Berlin.[8] The Soviet leader hoped the wall would prevent Westerners from having further influence on the East and halt the flow of refugees fleeing the Communist East.

Once again, Jack was bothered by his lack of clout and authority abroad. "We have a problem in making our power credible," he told a reporter that fall.[9] But something else was also affecting him as 1961 drew to a close—his father's health. On December 19, 73-year-old Joe Sr. suffered a massive stroke. It left him unable to speak and paralyzed on the right side of his body, though his mind continued to function. Joe Sr. would continue to live at the Kennedy compound in Hyannis Port until his death on November 18, 1969.

Politics at Home

While much of Jack's focus during his presidency was directed toward foreign policy, he also wanted to fix domestic problems. He took office during a recession, and business bankruptcies were at their highest level since the 1930s. More than 5.5 million Americans were unemployed.[10] In response, he put into place a series of measures designed to reverse the economic slump. He raised the minimum wage, which is the lowest hourly wage workers are permitted by law. And he used government funds to support local businesses and build affordable housing in poorer areas in order to stimulate public spending. By the end of Jack's first year, the recession had begun to decline.

One of Jack's first major successes was the creation of the Peace Corps. This government-backed organization inspired Americans to volunteer in developing nations across Latin America, Asia, and Africa. These volunteers provided aid or training in a wide range of fields, including medicine, education, farming, and construction. Since 1961, more than 168,000 citizens have participated in the program, working in more than 130 countries throughout the world.[13]

THE BIG MOMENT

THE CUBAN MISSILE CRISIS

In the early 1960s, tensions between the Soviet Union and the United States reached catastrophic levels. Due in part to the fallout from the failed Bay of Pigs invasion and the construction of the Berlin Wall, the possibility of a full-scale nuclear war seemed imminent.

On October 15, 1962, a U-2 spy plane took some alarming photographs. Despite Khrushchev's assurance the Soviet Union would not back Cuba in an armed attack, the pictures revealed the existence of Soviet bases in Cuba that housed nuclear missiles capable of striking major US cities. Jack knew something must be done. On October 22, he made a televised address to the nation in which he declared a naval blockade of Cuba. "Nuclear weapons are so destructive and ballistic missiles are so swift, that any substantially increased possibility of their use or any sudden change

A Soviet ship heads for Cuba on October 23.

in their deployment may well be regarded as a definite threat to peace," he said.[11]

Members of the United Nations Security Council recommended a preemptive attack, but Jack refused to launch an invasion. Finally, on October 28, Khrushchev agreed to remove the stockpile of missiles in exchange for assurances that the United States would not invade Cuba. In a separate deal that would remain secret from the public for 25 years, the US also agreed to remove its nuclear arsenal from Turkey. Thanks to Jack's convictions, another world war had, once again, been averted. "It is insane that two men, sitting on opposite sides of the world, should be able to decide to bring an end to civilization," Jack said later.[12]

Perhaps the most pressing domestic issue Jack faced during his presidency was civil rights. Though Jack had promised during his presidential campaign to be strong on racial issues, he shied away from advocating any major civil rights legislation while in office due to lack of public support. Instead, he focused on smaller successes. As part of an ongoing effort to stem segregation in restaurants, on buses, and in schools, his administration sent National Guard troops to accompany James Meredith, the first black student admitted to the all-white University of Mississippi, on his first day of classes in September 1962. Jack issued an executive order requiring federal agencies to hire minorities and appointed more than 40 African-American men and women to senior federal positions.[14] In response to bloody and violent white southern responses to civil rights marchers, Jack proposed a new civil rights bill to Congress on June 11, 1963. In his announcement of the bill, Jack said:

> It ought to be possible, in short, for every American to enjoy the privileges of being American without regard to his race or his color. . . . One hundred years of delay have passed since President Lincoln freed the slaves, yet their heirs, their grandsons, are not fully free.[15]

The proposed bill angered some of Jack's voters, especially conservatives in the South. Though the bill would not pass until Lyndon B. Johnson's administration,

Jack addresses 80 Peace Corps volunteers in August 1961.

NASA'S FIRST AFRICAN-AMERICAN ENGINEERS

In 1961, Jack issued an executive order requiring federal agencies to hire minorities. One of the first organizations to do so was NASA. Morgan Watson was one of the first African-American engineers at NASA. In an interview with National Public Radio, he recalled what the first few days of work were like: tense and awkward. But as African-American and white engineers began collaborating and getting along inside the office, some of the entrenched racial barriers and prejudices began falling away. "The space program certainly helped change the South," he said. "Not only NASA, but the whole federal government laid the groundwork for blacks to be integrated into the workplace."[16]

Jack's initial efforts set in motion some of the most sweeping changes in civil rights history.

Jack, Jackie, and their children, Caroline and John Jr., gather on Easter.

CHAPTER 6

JOHN F. KENNEDY
ASSASSINATED

It was a warm, sunny day on November 22, 1963, when Jack and the First Lady stepped off Air Force One at Love Field in Dallas, Texas. They were in Texas in advance of Jack's upcoming presidential reelection campaign, hoping to raise confidence in voters opposed to the civil rights bill. Grasping her husband's hand, Jackie—clad in a pale pink suit with matching pillbox hat and holding a bouquet of red roses—waved to the crowd as thousands clapped and cheered. It was one of the first times the couple had been seen together since the death of their third child, Patrick, who had died three months earlier, just two days after his birth.

Jack and Jackie arrive in Dallas on the morning of November 22.

> **"We cannot expect that everyone, to use the phrase of a decade ago, will 'talk sense to the American people.' But we can hope that fewer people will listen to nonsense. And the notion that this nation is headed for defeat through deficit, or that strength is but a matter of slogans, is nothing but just plain nonsense."[3]**
> *–John F. Kennedy, speech intended to be delivered on November 22, 1963*

The presidential motorcade was on its way to the Dallas Trade Mart, where Jack was scheduled to give a speech at 12:30 p.m. during a luncheon in his honor. He and Jackie were seated in the backseat of the convertible Lincoln limousine, while Texas Governor John Connally Jr. and his wife, Nellie, were riding in seats in front of them. Two Secret Service agents ran alongside the car. The protective bubble over the top of their car had been removed so he could see and be seen more easily. Gazing out at the hordes of people that lined the road in Dealey Plaza, Mrs. Connally turned to Jack and said, "Mr. President, you can't say Dallas doesn't love you."[1]

Suddenly, the sound of gunshots ricocheted through the air. The first bullet hit Jack in the throat. Then Governor Connally was struck in the back, chest, wrist, and thigh. "My God, I'm hit," the president moaned.[2] Because Jack was wearing a back brace that kept him upright, he could not slump over to safety. He was shot one final time in the back of the head.

Covered in blood, Jackie cradled her husband's battered head as the car raced to Parkland Memorial Hospital a few minutes away. An army of doctors and nurses did everything they could to repair the damage while Jackie stood waiting nearby. "The look in her eyes was like an animal that had been trapped, like a little rabbit—brave, but fear was in the eyes," remembered medical student David Edwards.[4] But it was hopeless. Twenty minutes after he arrived at the hospital, 46-year-old Jack was pronounced dead at 1:00 p.m. At 2:39 p.m. on Air Force One—with Jack's bronze coffin already on board—Vice President Johnson was sworn in as the thirty-sixth president of the United States.

Jackie stands by as Lyndon B. Johnson takes the oath of office hours after her husband was killed.

A Double Murder

Later that afternoon, his voice cracking, CBS newscaster Walter Cronkite interrupted the originally scheduled broadcast of the soap opera *As the World Turns* to inform the nation of Jack's death. It would be a charged moment people would remember for years to come. Why was the president shot? And how did the sniper, or snipers, get close enough to the president to shoot him without being caught?

The truth of what transpired that fateful afternoon came to light hours later. A 24-year-old ex-marine named Lee Harvey Oswald had been stationed at a window overlooking Dealey Plaza on the sixth floor of the Texas School Book Depository building. He had been hired there as a warehouse clerk one month earlier. As the president's motorcade rounded the corner onto Elm Street at 12:30 p.m., Oswald loaded his automatic rifle and pulled the trigger three times. Three minutes later, he left the building and stopped by the boardinghouse where he was living to pick up a revolver. Then, at 1:16 p.m., a patrol officer named J. D. Tippit was gunned down outside his police car a few minutes away. The culprit, whom witnesses identified as Tippit's shooter, was apprehended by police in the Texas Theater and taken into custody. That man, whom police soon came to believe also assassinated Jack, was Oswald.

For two days, the police interrogated Oswald about the double homicide. Having gotten wind of possible ties to Jack's murder, reporters streamed in and out of the jail where Oswald was being kept, snapping photos and recording footage. At 11:21 a.m. on the morning of November 24, something wholly unexpected happened. As Oswald was being transferred to the county jail, a 52-year-old nightclub owner named Jack Ruby, who had a previous arrest record and ties to the Mafia, reached for his gun and shot Oswald in the stomach. "You killed my president, you rat!" Ruby shouted as he pulled the trigger.[5]

The incident was broadcast live; millions of Americans who had been glued to the television since Jack's death witnessed the event as it unfolded.

LEE HARVEY OSWALD

Lee Harvey Oswald was born on October 18, 1939, in New Orleans, Louisiana. He spent part of his childhood in an orphanage before moving to New York City with his mother when he was 12. In 1956, 17-year-old Oswald enlisted in the marines. He was tried in a judicial court twice for owning a pistol and assaulting an officer. He became interested in Communism and tried to renounce his US citizenship to become a Soviet spy. He lived in the Soviet Union from 1960 to 1962 and married a Russian woman.

After moving with his wife to the United States in October 1962, Oswald became fascinated by the Communist revolution in Cuba and was critical of Jack's treatment of Castro. It was around this time he ordered rifles through the mail—one of which was used to kill Jack.

THE BIG MOMENT

WHAT ACTUALLY HAPPENED?

To this day, there are several conspiracy theories about what happened the day Jack was killed. In fact, a 2003 ABC News poll found 70 percent of Americans believe Jack's death was the result of a broader plot.[6] Though the Warren Commission, sanctioned by Lyndon B. Johnson, opened a lengthy investigation into the killings and ruled that Oswald acted alone, suspicions remain. Here are some of the theories:

The "Magic Bullet" Theory: If the Warren Commission's findings are correct, the first bullet that struck Jack entered through his back and out his throat. It then traveled to Governor Connally's back, up through his chest, and back down through his wrist and into his thigh, breaking two bones along the way. Is such a thing possible? Many conspiracy theorists insist the two men's wounds indicate the presence of multiple shooters.

Jackie leans over her husband as Secret Service agent Clinton Hill rides on the back of the convertible.

The Grassy Knoll: Did Oswald act alone? Some theorists believe another killer was hidden atop a nearby grassy knoll in Dealey Plaza. Maybe CIA agents killed Jack in retaliation for the Bay of Pigs. Or perhaps the mob hired Ruby to prevent Oswald from spilling the truth.

Zapruder's Film: Abraham Zapruder, a dress manufacturer who watched the motorcade, recorded the events using a home movie camera. The FBI confiscated the film soon after Jack was shot. Parts of the film were mysteriously destroyed while it was in the FBI's possession. What was on those missing segments?

Oswald never confessed to killing the president. He was pronounced dead at Parkland Memorial Hospital at 1:07 p.m. Ruby was found guilty of murder and sent to prison, where he died four years later of a blood clot in his lungs.

A Nation in Mourning

Jack's murder saddened Americans, and they mourned alongside the Kennedy family. Jack's body needed to be laid to rest. On November 24, Jack's coffin, draped in an American flag, was placed on a platform in the Capitol Rotunda—the same spot where Abraham Lincoln's body was held a century prior in 1865. Hundreds of thousands of mourners from across the country came to pay their respects to the fallen leader.[7]

The following morning, dressed in a black suit with a black veil draped over her face, 34-year-old Jackie kneeled and kissed her husband's casket. Then she and Jack's remaining brothers—Bobby and Ted—walked the eight blocks to Saint Matthew's Cathedral following the horse-drawn funeral procession as more than one million onlookers lined the street and 175 million tuned in on television.[8] Black Jack, a riderless horse, trailed close behind, and the sound of bagpipes filled the air.

Members of the military carry Jack's coffin from Saint Matthew's Cathedral in Washington.

A PHOTOGRAPH TO REMEMBER

Out of all of the 70 press photographers covering Jack's funeral, United Press International photographer Stan Stearns happened to capture the iconic shot of John Jr.—whose third birthday was the same day as the funeral—saluting his father's coffin as it made its way toward Arlington National Cemetery.

"As the [casket] was rolling out to Arlington Cemetery, I asked every photographer I could if they had the salute. Duh! Nobody saw it," Stearns later recalled. "Everyone I talked to had been concentrating on Jackie and the [casket]."

In a split-second decision, he skipped the funeral and raced back to UPI's darkroom to develop the film. His boss was furious. "The bureau chief almost had a hemorrhage," Stearns said. "I never saw a man turn as white as he did because I was not with the entourage going to Arlington."[9] But in the end, Stearns's photo was the one that made history.

After the hour-long Mass, the procession headed toward Arlington National Cemetery. Fifty jet fighters flew above the cemetery in a V formation, and a bugle played a somber melody as Jack's coffin was lowered into the ground at 3:32 p.m. With tears in her eyes, Jackie took a candle and lit the eternal flame that burns next to Jack's gravesite to this day. Later that evening, accompanied by two Secret Service agents, Bobby and Jackie made the trip back to the cemetery without the crowds.

Nearly one year after Jack's funeral, the report of the Warren Commission—an 889-page document detailing the findings of a full investigation into what actually happened in Dallas—was published on September 24, 1964. It confirmed Oswald was the sole killer. It did not change the fact that Jack was gone. But he would never be forgotten.

John Jr. salutes his father's casket.

CHAPTER 7

BOBBY TAKES
THE REINS

It was now up to 38-year-old Bobby to uphold the Kennedy name and reputation. He had gained valuable experience early on in his career as a lawyer for the US Department of Justice. In 1953, he identified Communist sympathizers in his role as assistant counsel for the Permanent Subcommittee on Investigations, led by anticommunist crusader Senator Joseph McCarthy. Bobby also served for three years as attorney general while Jack was president, fighting organized crime and crooked labor unions, gathering support for the proposed Civil Rights Act of 1964, and advising his brother on all matters of government. With both of his older brothers dead, it was Bobby's turn to lead.

Bobby, Ethel, and seven of their kids

> "I happen to believe that the 1954 [Supreme Court school desegregation] decision was right. But my belief does not matter. It is the law. Some of you may believe the decision was wrong. That does not matter. It is the law."[2]
>
> —*Robert F. Kennedy, in a 1961 speech at the University of Georgia Law School*

The political and economic climate Bobby faced in 1963 was full of turmoil and violence. Medgar Evers, a Mississippi field secretary for the National Association for the Advancement of Colored People, was murdered by white segregationist Byron De La Beckwith in his driveway on June 12, just two months before civil rights leader Reverend Dr. Martin Luther King Jr. delivered his famous "I Have a Dream" speech during the March on Washington. More than 16,000 US troops had been deployed to Vietnam to fight a civil war. This decision divided the country. The gap between the rich and poor was still overwhelming, and unemployment held steady at 6 percent.[1]

Bobby was suffering from personal pressures, too. He was married to his sister Jean's no-nonsense Manhattanville College roommate, Ethel Skakel, and the proud father of eight children—they eventually would have 11 children total. But Bobby grew depressed after Jack's death. He adopted many of Jack's mannerisms, cried openly in public, and took frequent trips from his family's estate in McLean, Virginia, to visit Jack's grave with Jackie. Because of his sadness, Bobby was having difficulty visualizing what his future might look like. Journalist Jack Newfield wrote,

The assassination punctured the center of Robert Kennedy's universe. It removed the hero-brother for whom he had submerged all of his own great competitive instincts. It took away, in one instant of insanity, all of the power [the brothers] had struggled together for ten years to achieve.[3]

For the first time in his life, it was essential that Bobby figure out what he believed in and decide what he wanted to do next. He toyed briefly with becoming Johnson's running mate in the 1964 presidential election. But when Johnson ruled out any possibility of a cabinet member doing so, Bobby set his course on a different path. Similar to his 32-year-old brother Ted, who was first elected to a US Senate seat one year earlier on November 7, 1962, Bobby decided to run for the US Senate.

Bobby's Senate Term

In 1964, Bobby resigned as attorney general in order to campaign for a New York Senate

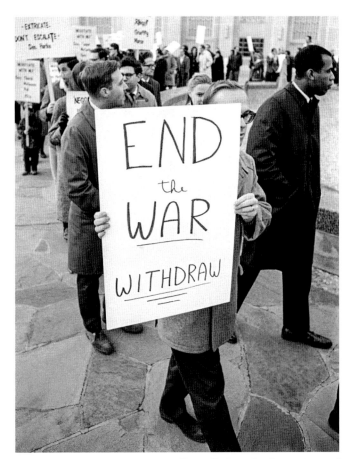

Demonstrators march at Indiana University in protest of the Vietnam War.

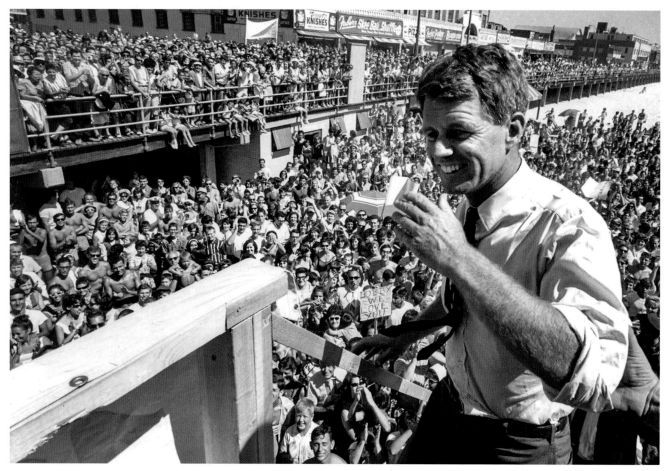

Bobby prepares to give a speech to a crowd in New York during his Senate campaign.

seat. Though some critics dubbed him an outsider because of his lack of connection to New York or its politics, Bobby beat out incumbent Kenneth Keating, a Republican, by nearly 719,000 votes.[4] For the next four years in the Senate, Bobby concentrated on two issues of utmost importance to Americans at the time: poverty and inequality.

From 1965 to 1967, Bobby traveled to far-flung regions of the country and abroad to advocate for those less fortunate and to study the impact of poverty on culture. In 1966, he sponsored an amendment to the Economic Opportunity Act of 1964. This allowed for a program that would use federal funds for urban development projects in underserved communities across the United States, providing jobs and social services for those in need. Founded in 1967, his Bedford Stuyvesant Renewal and Rehabilitation Corporation in Brooklyn was one of the first successes of the program and served as a model for other initiatives nationwide. Bobby remarked in a speech on January 20, 1967:

> The plight of the cities—the physical decay and human despair that pervades them—is the great internal problem of the American nation, a challenge which must be met. The peculiar genius of America has been its ability, in the face of such challenges, to summon all our resources of mind and body, to focus these resources, and our attention and effort, in whatever amount is necessary to solve the deepest and most resistant problems. That is the commitment and the spirit required in our cities today.[5]

During that time period, Bobby also made strides to improve conditions in rural areas for racial minorities from Appalachia to the West. Though he "was hated by the powerful southern faction within the party, distrusted by many liberals, opposed by organized labor, resented by Democratic loyalists for fracturing party unity," and

THE BEDFORD STUYVESANT RENEWAL AND REHABILITATION CORPORATION

In the 1960s, the Bedford-Stuyvesant neighborhood in Brooklyn, New York, left a lot to be desired. Schools floundered, housing projects were in disrepair, and minorities were overlooked among their rich, white neighbors. When Bobby visited the area in 1967, civil rights activists challenged him to go beyond his speeches and find a solution for the problems there.

With the help of New York Senator Jacob Javits, Bobby gutted an abandoned milk-bottling plant to create the Bedford Stuyvesant Restoration Corporation, one of the first organizations of its kind focused on improving conditions in impoverished communities. It housed classrooms for job training courses, and during the early 1970s, after Bobby's death, government-subsidized apartment buildings were built on the property. Those developments still exist to this day.

"[Bobby] really came with an eye of interest, and we were pleased that he did," activist Elsie Richardson told the *New York Times*. "It did a lot for the neighborhood. The neighborhood developed a spirit of being able to do things for itself."[7]

often butted heads with President Johnson, Bobby refused to back down in his zealous approach to helping the disenfranchised.[6] He supported union leader and National Farm Workers Association cofounder Cesar Chavez in his efforts to unionize migrant laborers, backed raising education standards for Native American children on reservations, and lobbied Congress to revise the federal food stamps program for low-income African Americans in the Mississippi Delta.

As his first term as a New York senator wound down, Bobby was fed up with Johnson. No longer content to exert his influence in Congress, Bobby decided to run for president.

An Unfitting End

On March 16, 1968, Bobby announced his candidacy for the presidential nomination. He ran on an antiwar platform as a socially progressive Democrat, pushing many of the issues he supported as a senator. When President Johnson pulled out of the race on March 31, leaving liberal Eugene McCarthy and Vice President Hubert Humphrey still in the running, Bobby felt he had a chance of winning. For the next three months, he campaigned nonstop and won primaries in Nebraska, Indiana, and California. Little did he know the contest in California would be his last.

BOBBY'S STANCE ON THE VIETNAM WAR

When Bobby was first elected to the Senate, he supported President Johnson's stance on Vietnam—a situation Johnson had inherited from Jack. As time wore on and the number of US soldiers in Vietnam grew to more than 385,300 by the end of 1966, Bobby began to oppose the bombing of North Vietnam.[8] When Johnson refused to stop the bombing, Bobby formally broke with President Johnson in 1966. "Are we like the God of the Old Testament that we can decide, in Washington, DC, what cities, what towns, what hamlets in Vietnam are going to be destroyed?" Bobby asked in a 1967 speech. "Do we have to accept that? . . . I do not think we have to."[9]

On the morning of June 5, 1968, after giving a speech in Los Angeles celebrating his California win, Bobby was shot three times in a kitchen corridor outside the ballroom of the Ambassador Hotel by a 24-year-old Palestinian immigrant named Sirhan Bishara Sirhan. As at the time of Jack's assassination nearly five years earlier, surgeons did everything they could to save Bobby's life, but to no avail. He died at 1:44 a.m. on June 6 at the age of 42.

SIRHAN SIRHAN

Sirhan Bishara Sirhan, a Palestinian immigrant born in Jerusalem in 1944, moved to California with his family as a boy. He stated he murdered Bobby because the senator supported Israel in the Arab-Israeli War of 1967. On April 23, 1969, Sirhan was given the death penalty. Sirhan's sentence was changed to life in prison when the California Supreme Court abolished the death penalty in 1972. As of August 2015, the 71-year-old Sirhan is still in jail.

Bobby's body was flown from California to New York's Saint Patrick's Cathedral on June 6. More than 100,000 people came to view the flag-draped coffin, some waiting in line for hours to pay their respects.[10] The casket then made its final journey to Arlington National Cemetery by train. The 225-mile (362 km) trip took more than eight hours—twice the usual time as hundreds of thousands of grievers lined the tracks and slowed the train's progress. "I seen people running all over! They were running toward the train. They tried to touch the train as it went by," an

Crowds gather to pay their respects to Bobby as his body travels by train to Arlington National Cemetery.

electrician told a reporter. "People were praying. The men had their hats off. They were crossing themselves. . . . The signs read, WHO WILL BE THE NEXT ONE? and WE HAVE LOST OUR LAST HOPE," a train conductor said.[11]

Across the world, millions mourned as another Kennedy was laid to rest later that evening—the fourth of Joe Sr. and Rose's children to die. It was now up to the youngest Kennedy—Ted—to carry the political torch forward.

CHAPTER 8

TED'S CAREER IN
THE SENATE

In the summer of 1968, 36-year-old Senator Ted Kennedy was wracked with grief over the gruesome deaths of his siblings—first Joe Jr., Kick, Jack, and now Bobby. Four years earlier, Ted had experienced his own near-fatal brush with fate. A small two-engine plane carrying him and four other passengers from Washington, DC, to Westfield, Massachusetts, crashed into an orchard three miles (4.8 km) short of the runway on June 19, 1964. Though two people died in the accident, Ted survived, with a five-month hospital stay to fix three broken vertebrae, two broken ribs, a broken back, and a collapsed lung. He had escaped "the Kennedy curse"—but barely.[1]

Ted needed time to grieve his siblings before returning to his political career.

THE KENNEDY CURSE

The Kennedys are one of the most legendary families in US history. Historians and media personalities have long wondered if the Kennedys are afflicted by the curse of dying unnaturally young. Here are a few of the tragedies that afflicted the family in later years.

- April 25, 1984: 29-year-old David Kennedy, the fourth of Bobby's 11 children, died in a Florida hotel room from a drug overdose.

- December 31, 1997: 39-year-old Michael Kennedy, the sixth of Bobby's children, was killed in a skiing accident in Colorado.

- July 16, 1999: 38-year-old John F. Kennedy Jr., Jack's only son, and his wife Carolyn died in a plane crash near Martha's Vineyard, Massachusetts.

- May 16, 2012: 52-year-old Mary Kennedy, the estranged wife of Robert Kennedy Jr., committed suicide.

For weeks after Bobby's murder, Ted kept out of the public eye and considered retiring from political life altogether. He went sailing by himself in Hyannis Port and took many long drives. He became a surrogate father for Ethel and Bobby's children. After two months, he gave a speech announcing his intentions to return to Washington.

There is no safety in hiding, so today, I resume my public responsibilities to the people of Massachusetts. Like my three brothers before me, I pick up a fallen standard. Sustained by the memory of our priceless years together, I shall try to carry forward that special commitment to justice, to excellence, to courage that distinguished their lives.[2]

Trouble Ahead

Though Ted had not yet announced his intention to run, he began acting as though a future presidential campaign might be a possibility. Similar to his brother Bobby, Ted was outspoken in his disdain for US involvement in Vietnam and advocated hard for the repeal of the draft. In 1969, the 37-year-old became the youngest-ever majority whip in the Senate, charged with mobilizing votes within the Democratic Party on major issues. But underneath Ted's assured exterior, a reckless streak threatened to bubble over and ruin his political career.

For years, rumors of Ted's extramarital affairs had circulated in the media. His incessant quest for fun had threatened an already deteriorating marriage to his first wife, Joan. Between Joan's alcoholism and Ted's wayward behavior, Kara, Edward Jr., and Patrick, the couple's three young children, suffered. "There was a general feeling that Ted was a playboy—he drove too fast, he drank too much, he chased girls," recalled Richard Hardwood, a reporter from the *Washington Post*. "He certainly was devoted to Ethel Kennedy and her family, but he was having problems of his own."[3]

On July 18, 1969, Ted's carousing came to a head. After a cookout for Ted's campaign secretaries on Chappaquiddick Island, Ted accidentally drove his car off a narrow bridge. Though he managed to swim to safety, the girl he was with, 28-year-old Mary Jo Kopechne, did not survive the crash. Ted waited to report the incident for ten hours, until the next morning. By then, it was too late. Two boys on an early morning fishing excursion discovered the waterlogged car. The Chappaquiddick police were called, and Kopechne's body was removed from the wreckage.

The vehicle Ted was driving was pulled from the water after going off a bridge.

One week later, Ted pleaded guilty for leaving the scene of the accident in exchange for a reduced sentence: a two-month jail term, which was later suspended. He gave a speech on national television to 35 million viewers, admitting he was "overcome . . . by a jumble of emotion—grief, fear, doubt, exhaustion, panic, confusion, and shock."[4] But the damage had been done. Ted would soon return to the Senate. But all hope for becoming the 1972 Democratic candidate for president had vanished.

The Lion of the Senate

With the Kopechne scandal still raw and the death of his father Joe Sr. four months later, on November 18, 1969, Ted hit rock bottom. Though he made a concerted effort to turn his life around, troubles in his personal life continued to haunt him for years. In 1980, he tried unsuccessfully for the Democratic nomination for president, losing 24 out of 34 primaries to incumbent Jimmy Carter.[5] In 1982, after

"The [Kennedy] legacy has to be an enormous burden. Who would want to be in a position of having to live your life with the feeling that, if you didn't become president of the United States and fulfill all of these enormous hopes that had been raised by your brothers—who never had a chance to fulfill them—that somehow people would judge your life, or you might judge it yourself to be a failure? I can't conceive of a greater or more difficult burden to carry."[6]

—Adam Walinsky, legislative assistant to Bobby Kennedy

24 years of marriage, he and Joan divorced, citing irreparable differences. He married Victoria Ann Reggie, a Washington lawyer, in 1992 and became a stepfather to her two children, Curran and Caroline Raclin.

Despite never becoming president, Ted's career in the Senate—the fourth longest in US history—blossomed into an impressive legacy that shaped government policies for more than four decades, through Jack's presidency in 1962 to that of Barack Obama in 2009. During the 1970s, under Presidents Richard Nixon, Gerald Ford, and Jimmy Carter, Ted was instrumental in winning the fight in Congress for allowing 18-year-olds to vote, abolishing the military draft, deregulating the airline and trucking industries, and establishing the Occupational Safety and Health Administration (OSHA) to monitor workplace safety compliance.

During the 1980s and 1990s, Ted became even more outspoken about his liberal-leaning views, earning him the title "the Lion of the Senate."[7] He prevented the Reagan administration from weakening the Voting Rights Act of 1965, an act that reduced barriers preventing African Americans from voting. In 1990, under President George H. W. Bush, he pushed through Congress the Americans with Disabilities Act, which prohibits discrimination against people with disabilities in employment, transportation, and public accommodation. And Ted endorsed the groundbreaking State Children's Health Insurance Program (CHIP). Since its creation in 1997, CHIP has allocated more than $20 billion to help states insure more than 8 million children whose low-income families are ineligible for Medicaid but cannot afford private insurance.[8]

"[Ted] has one of the most distinguished alumni associations of any US senator," Rutgers University political scientist Ross K. Baker told the *New York Times*. "To have served in even a minor capacity in the Kennedy office or on one of his committees is a major entry in anyone's résumé."[9]

A LONG-TERM LEGACY

According to Vincent Bzdek, author of *The Kennedy Legacy: Jack, Bobby and Ted and a Family Dream Fulfilled*, Ted spent more than 17,000 days in the US Senate, cast more than 15,000 votes, and wrote more than 2,500 bills during his career.[10]

The Senate Loses a Legend

On May 17, 2008, just four months after he endorsed Barack Obama for president, Ted was diagnosed with a brain tumor. One year later, during President Obama's post-inauguration luncheon, Ted suffered a seizure, and his health declined rapidly thereafter. In the last ten years of his Senate career, Ted had become renowned for reaching across the aisle to work with Republicans on health-care reform and expanding Medicaid coverage, passing the No Child Left Behind Act in 2001, and sponsoring the bipartisan Bioterrorism Preparedness and Response Act in 2002.

PATIENT PROTECTION AND AFFORDABLE CARE ACT

Near the end of his life, Ted did all he could to reform health care in the United States. As chairman of the Health, Education, Labor, and Pensions (HELP) Committee until his death, he was an outspoken leader in shepherding President Obama's Affordable Care Act through Congress. In 2009, HELP drafted the Affordable Health Choices Act—a precursor to the Affordable Care Act, legislation that would "provide quality, affordable health care for all Americans and enshrine a patients' bill of rights into law."[12] Though the Affordable Care Act would not pass until March 23, 2010, after Ted's death, the senator was instrumental in paving the way for its success.

On August 25, 2009, after 46 long years and nine terms in the Senate, 77-year-old Ted died at his Cape Cod, Massachusetts, home surrounded by his family.

"[Ted Kennedy] deserves recognition not just as the leading senator of his time, but as one of the greats in its history, wise in the workings of this singular institution, especially its demand to be more than partisan," biographer Adam Clymer wrote in *Edward M. Kennedy: A Biography*. "The deaths and tragedies around him would have led others to withdraw. He never [quit], but [sailed] against the wind."[11]

Ted served his country proudly in the Senate for decades before passing away.

CHAPTER 9

THE KENNEDY LEGACY

Unlike in countries such as the United Kingdom, Spain, Thailand, or Japan, royalty does not exist in the United States. But with at least one descendant in some form of political office for more than 68 years, Joe Sr. and Rose gave birth to a political dynasty that captured the public's attention and helped shape the course of history perhaps more than any other family in US politics. In the years following Jack's presidency, journalists began referring to the Kennedys as "Camelot" after King Arthur's legendary court. The name was inspired by Jackie and presidential adviser Ted Sorensen as a way to sustain the legacy of Jack's administration. "They are America's family," said Boston University historian Thomas Whalen. "Both good and bad."[1]

The Kennedy family captured the attention of the American public for decades.

BOBBY KENNEDY'S INFLUENCE

Kathleen Kennedy Townsend, Bobby Kennedy's oldest child, remembers her father's return home from the Mississippi Delta after traveling there to study poverty. She says he was 'very much stunned and shocked' by what he saw. "Do you know how lucky you are?" he asked her at the time. "Do something for your country."[2]

In fact, most of Bobby and Ethel's children ended up following that advice. Robert Jr. is an environmental lawyer and founder of the Waterkeeper Alliance. Mary Kerry established the Robert F. Kennedy Center for Human Rights. She is an international human rights activist. And Rory is an award-winning filmmaker who has made documentaries about Vietnam and Iraq's Abu Ghraib prison.

Perpetuating the Camelot Myth

Though none of the subsequent generations of Kennedys have achieved political success on par with Jack, Bobby, and Teddy, a number of younger family members threw their hats in the political ring with varying degrees of success. Mark Kennedy Shriver, son of Eunice Kennedy and Robert Sargent Shriver Jr., served in the Maryland House of Delegates from 1995 to 2003. In 2002, he ran for a House of Representatives seat but was defeated in the Democratic primary.

Kathleen Kennedy Townsend, Bobby and Ethel's eldest daughter, was lieutenant governor of Maryland from 1995 to 2003 before moving on to become an attorney. Bobby's eldest son, Joseph Patrick Kennedy II, served as a member of the US House of Representatives from the eighth congressional district of Massachusetts from 1987 to 1999. And Caroline Bouvier Kennedy, Jack and Jackie's only daughter, attempted to run for her uncle's old New York Senate seat in 2008 but withdrew her candidacy after a poorly run campaign knocked her out of the running. She served as President Obama's ambassador to Japan.

Perhaps the person with the most responsibility for carrying on the Kennedy political legacy is Bobby Kennedy's grandson Joseph P. Kennedy III. Born in Massachusetts in 1980, he was elected to the Massachusetts House of Representatives in 2012, replacing the retiring legislator Democrat Barney Frank. Similar to his father, Joseph P. Kennedy II, and great-uncle Ted, Joe III leans toward the liberal side of politics. He supports gay marriage, is pro-choice on abortion,

MORE KENNEDY SCANDALS

The Kennedys were infamous for attracting scandals, and the gossip mill did not stop turning once the younger generations came of age. Some of the most scandalous stories include one about Bobby's son Douglas kicking a nurse in 2012 as she tried to stop him from taking his baby out of a hospital. And Douglas's brother Michael reportedly had an affair with his family's teenage babysitter before he died in 1997.

endorses the Affordable Care Act, and is a strong proponent of increasing the country's reliance on renewable energy.

An Artistic Bunch

For as many Kennedys who have gone into some form of public service, there are just as many who shied away from the field altogether. *Washington Post* editor and Kennedy biographer Bzdek suggests it is because they are scarred by the tragedies that stalked their fathers and uncles. "There's a real sentiment among this generation that they paid too high a price for their public service. There's less talent and ability in this generation, but there's also less willingness to do whatever it takes," he says.[3]

With an eye for art and culture, some Kennedys and their cousins followed a creative path. Christopher Kennedy Lawford, son of Patricia Kennedy, became a writer and actor. Amanda Mary Smith, Jean Ann's daughter, published *Hostage to Fortune: The Letters of Joseph P. Kennedy* in 2001. Kara Anne, Ted and Joan's daughter, produced films for Very Special Arts, an organization for people with disabilities, and was a director emeritus of the John F. Kennedy Presidential Library and Museum until she died from a heart attack in 2011. Maria Shriver, former First Lady of California as the then wife of former California governor Arnold Schwarzenegger, published six books and was a network news correspondent and anchor for CBS and NBC.

The most recent generation of Kennedys is an artistic bunch, too. Kathleen Kennedy, Bobby's 27-year-old granddaughter, became an actress and starred on *The Newsroom* in 2012. Bobby Kennedy III wrote and directed a one-act comedic documentary called "ELEW-Live from Infinity" in 2011. And in 2010, 21-year-old Katherine Schwarzenegger published *Rock What You've Got: Secrets to Loving Your Inner and Outer Beauty from Someone Who's Been There and Back*, a self-help book about body issues.

Whether or not another Kennedy will reach the heights of political fame and fortune—or experience the tragic lows—that Jack, Bobby, or Ted did remains to be seen. Only time will tell. For now, the long arms of Joe and Rose Kennedy reach forward into a new era—embracing, manipulating, and shaping the historic changes to come.

Television Academy | HONORS

Although not in politics herself, Shriver has done a lot of public work.

1888

Joseph P. Kennedy is born.

1914

Joe and Rose Fitzgerald are married on October 7 and move to 83 Beals Street in Brookline, Massachusetts.

1917

John F. "Jack" Kennedy is born on May 29; Joe Sr. is introduced to Franklin D. Roosevelt.

1925

Robert R. "Bobby" Kennedy is born on November 20.

1932

Edward "Ted" Kennedy is born on February 22.

1934

Joe Sr. serves as chairman of the Securities and Exchange Commission under President Roosevelt.

1938

Joe Sr. becomes the US ambassador to the United Kingdom; the Kennedys move into a mansion in London.

1940

Joe Sr. resigns as ambassador because of his unpopular beliefs about World War II.

1944

Kick marries Lord William Cavendish Hartington on May 6; Joe Jr. is killed during a dangerous pilot mission on August 12.

1946

Jack is elected to his first of three terms in Massachusetts's eleventh congressional district seat.

1952

Jack wins a US Senate seat; He serves as senator from Massachusetts until 1960.

1953

Jack marries Jacqueline Bouvier on September 12.

1960

Jack is elected the thirty-fifth president of the United States on November 8.

1962

Ted is elected to the Senate in November, where he will serve for the next 46 years.

1963

Alleged sniper Lee Harvey Oswald assassinates President Kennedy on November 22 in Dallas, Texas; On November 25, Jack's body is laid to rest in Arlington National Cemetery.

1964

Bobby resigns as attorney general and runs successfully in New York for a US Senate seat, where he will serve for four years.

1968

Bobby announces his candidacy for the presidency but is assassinated by Sirhan Sirhan on June 5; he dies the following day.

1987

Joseph Patrick Kennedy II, son of Bobby Kennedy, is elected to Congress from the eighth congressional district of Massachusetts, where he will serve until 1999.

2012

Joseph P. Kennedy III is elected to the US House of Representatives for Massachusetts's fourth congressional district, following in his uncle Ted's footsteps.

In 1965, after his brother was killed, Bobby Kennedy climbed a mountain in the Canadian Yukon on an expedition sponsored by the National Geographic Society. At the time, the 14,000-foot (4,267 m) mountain had yet to be summited—Bobby was the first to do so. Afterward, the mountain was named Mount Kennedy to honor Jack Kennedy.

While at Harvard, Ted Kennedy excelled at football. He was so talented he was recruited by the Green Bay Packers in 1955. Ted went to Virginia Law School instead, where he graduated in 1959.

During Jack's tenure in the Oval Office, John Jr. liked to play under his father's desk. There was a secret door in the desk that he used to hide inside and pop out at random times.

Joe Kennedy amassed a huge fortune that he passed on to his children. So when Jack entered Congress in 1947, he decided to donate his salary to charity—a practice he continued to follow as president.

During her husband's presidency, Jackie Kennedy tried to shield her two children from the media. She turned the White House's third floor into a nursery school with teachers. She even invited some of the Kennedy staffers' kids to attend.

In 1975, following the death of her second husband, Aristotle Onassis, Jackie moved to New York to become a book editor.

Caroline Kennedy was allowed to keep a pony at the White House. She named it Macaroni.

Jackie Kennedy was multilingual. In addition to English, she also spoke French, Spanish, and Italian.

After Barack Obama's election night promise to buy his two daughters a puppy, Ted Kennedy gave them a Portuguese water dog as a gift instead. He even took Bo, the First Dog, to his preferred trainer in Virginia.

appeasement

The policy of granting concessions to potential enemies to maintain peace.

attorney general

The head of the US Department of Justice and a member of the president's cabinet.

bipartisan

Relating to or involving the cooperation of two political parties that generally oppose one another.

cabinet

A group of presidential advisers.

conservative

One who believes in established, traditional values in politics, marked by moderation and caution, and resistance to change.

debutant

A person who is making a first appearance.

defect

To leave a country or political party and join a competing one.

deficit

The excess of spending and liabilities over revenue and assets.

dynasty

A family or group that maintains power for several generations.

governess

A woman who is paid to care for and teach a child in the child's house.

inauguration

A formal induction into office.

incumbent

An official currently in office.

liberal

One who is open to new ideas and ways of thinking, and who believes the government should be active in supporting social and political change.

motorcade

A procession of motor vehicles, as in a parade.

Pulitzer Prize

Any of several awards established by Joseph Pulitzer and conferred annually for accomplishment in various fields of American journalism, literature, and music.

recession

A period of time during which the economy slows down, including a decline in trade and industrial activity and the loss of jobs.

segregation

The practice of separating people of different races, classes, or ethnic groups, as in schools, housing, and public or commercial facilities.

stock market

The market in which stocks are bought and sold, usually including the organized exchanges and over-the-counter markets in a particular country or economic region.

surrogate

One that takes the place of another.

SELECTED BIBLIOGRAPHY

Hunt, Amber, and David Batcher. *The Kennedy Wives: Triumph and Tragedy in America's Most Public Family.* Guilford, CT: Lyons Press, 2014. Print.

Maier, Thomas. *The Kennedys: America's Emerald Kings.* New York: Basic, 2003. Print.

"The Presidents: The Kennedys." *American Experience.* PBS. WGBH, Boston. 2008. Television.

Willis, Clint, Ed. *Kennedys: Stories of Life and Death from an American Family.* New York: Thunder's Mouth Press, 2001. Print.

FURTHER READINGS

Mara, Wil. *The Assassination of President John F. Kennedy.* New York: Franklin Watts, 2015. Print.

Norwich, Grace. *I Am John F. Kennedy.* New York: Scholastic, 2013. Print.

Swanson, James L. *"The President Has Been Shot:" The Assassination of John F. Kennedy.* New York: Scholastic, 2013. Print.

WEBSITES

To learn more about America's Great Political Families, visit **booklinks.abdopublishing.com**. These links are routinely monitored and updated to provide the most current information available.

JOHN F. KENNEDY NATIONAL HISTORIC SITE

83 Beals Street

Brookline, MA 02446

617-566-7937

http://www.nps.gov/jofi/index.htm

Come see Joseph P. Kennedy and Rose Fitzgerald's first home together—the birthplace of President John F. Kennedy. The quaint house is filled with period furniture, old photographs, and charm.

JOHN F. KENNEDY PRESIDENTIAL LIBRARY AND MUSEUM

220 Morrissey Boulevard

Boston, MA 02125

617-514-1600

http://www.jfklibrary.org

This museum is packed with photos and videos from John F. Kennedy's life and memorabilia documenting his family's legacy, while the Presidential Library has more than 400 collections of personal papers and records.

SOURCE NOTES

CHAPTER 1. ELECTION NIGHT 1960

1. David Von Pein's JFK Channel. "Election Night 1960 NBC-TV Coverage." Online video clip. *YouTube.* YouTube, 30 Aug. 2013. Web. 5 Aug. 2015.

2. "Magnetic Tape Station for the RCA 501 Computer." *Smithsonian.* Smithsonian, n.d. Web. 5 Aug. 2015.

3. "Campaign of 1960." *John F. Kennedy Presidential Library and Museum.* John F. Kennedy Presidential Library and Museum, n.d. Web. 5 Aug. 2015.

4. James Reston. "Kennedy's Victory Won By Close Margin; He Promises Fight for World Freedom; Eisenhower Offers 'Orderly Transition.'" *New York Times.* New York Times Company, 10 Nov. 1960. Web. 5 Aug. 2015.

5. Ibid.

6. "1960 Presidential Election Returns." *John F. Kennedy Presidential Library and Museum.* John F. Kennedy Presidential Library and Museum, n.d. Web. 5 Aug. 2015.

CHAPTER 2. THE PATRIARCH

1. Patricia Brennan. "The Kennedys." *Washington Post.* Washington Post, 20 Sept. 1992. Web. 5 Aug. 2015.

2. Amber Hunt and David Batcher. *The Kennedy Wives: Triumph and Tragedy in America's Most Public Family.* Guilford, CT: Lyons, 2014. Print. 4.

3. "The Presidents: The Kennedys." *American Experience.* PBS. WGBH, Boston. 2008. Television.

4. Amber Hunt and David Batcher. *The Kennedy Wives: Triumph and Tragedy in America's Most Public Family.* Guilford, CT: Lyons, 2014. Print. 7–9.

5. Ibid. 10.

6. "Joseph P. Kennedy." *John F. Kennedy Presidential Library and Museum.* John F. Kennedy Presidential Library and Museum, n.d. Web. 5 Aug. 2015.

7. "The Presidents: The Kennedys." *American Experience.* PBS. WGBH, Boston. 2008. Television.

8. Michael O'Brien. *John F. Kennedy: A Biography.* New York: St. Martin's, 2005. Print. 22.

CHAPTER 3. THE KENNEDYS AT WAR

1. Amber Hunt and David Batcher. *The Kennedy Wives: Triumph and Tragedy in America's Most Public Family.* Guilford, CT: Lyons, 2014. Print. 28.

2. "Primary Resources: Is Democracy Finished?" *American Experience.* WGBH, 2013. Web. 5 Aug. 2015.

3. "Rosemary Kennedy." *John F. Kennedy Presidential Library and Museum.* John F. Kennedy Presidential Library and Museum, n.d. Web. 5 Aug. 2015.

4. "History of Special Olympics." *Special Olympics.* Special Olympics, 2015. Web. 5 Aug. 2015.

5. Amber Hunt and David Batcher. *The Kennedy Wives: Triumph and Tragedy in America's Most Public Family.* Guilford, CT: Lyons, 2014. Print. 36.

6. Joseph M. Siracusa. *Encyclopedia of the Kennedys: The People and Events that Shaped America.* Santa Barbara, CA: ABC-CLIO, 2012. Print. 420.

CHAPTER 4. A BID FOR THE PRESIDENCY

1. "The Presidents: The Kennedys." *American Experience.* PBS. WGBH, Boston. 2008. Television.

2. Ibid.

3. "Results of John F. Kennedy's 1946 US Congressional Election." *John F. Kennedy Presidential Library and Museum.* John F. Kennedy Presidential Library and Museum, n.d. Web. 5 Aug. 2015.

4. Vincent Bzdek. *The Kennedy Legacy: Jack, Bobby and Ted and a Family Dream Fulfilled.* New York: Palgrave Macmillan, 2009. Print. 70.

5. "The Presidents: The Kennedys." *American Experience.* PBS. WGBH, Boston. 2008. Television.

6. Gloria Negri. "Pauline Fitzgerald; The Force behind Famed JFK Tea Parties." *Boston.com.* New York Times Company, 18 Feb. 2008. Web. 5 Aug. 2015.

7. "Photos: JFK and Jackie's Wedding, 1953." *Life.* Time, 2014. Web. 5 Aug. 2015.

8. Amber Hunt and David Batcher. *The Kennedy Wives: Triumph and Tragedy in America's Most Public Family.* Guilford, CT: Lyons, 2014. Print. 149.

9. Ibid. 185.

10. Plasma Ben. "JFK—We Choose to Go to the Moon, Full Length." Online video clip. *YouTube.* YouTube, 27 Aug. 2008. Web. 5 Aug. 2015.

11. "Campaign of 1960." *John F. Kennedy Presidential Library and Museum.* John F. Kennedy Presidential Library and Museum, n.d. Web. 5 Aug. 2015.

12. "The Presidents: The Kennedys." *American Experience.* PBS. WGBH, Boston. 2008. Television.

13. Max Power. "Frank Sinatra—'High Hopes' with Jack Kennedy (1960)." Online video clip. *YouTube.* YouTube, 23 Feb. 2010. Web. 5 Aug. 2015.

14. "The Kennedy-Nixon Debates." *History.* A&E Television Networks, 18 Nov. 2013. Web. 5 Aug. 2015.

15. "The Presidents: The Kennedys." *American Experience.* PBS. WGBH, Boston. 2008. Television.

CHAPTER 5. A KENNEDY IN THE WHITE HOUSE

1. "John F. Kennedy Quotations." *John F. Kennedy Presidential Library and Museum.* John F. Kennedy Presidential Library and Museum, n.d. Web. 5 Aug. 2015.

2. Ibid.

3. "The Bay of Pigs." *John F. Kennedy Presidential Library and Museum.* John F. Kennedy Presidential Library and Museum, n.d. Web. 5 Aug. 2015.

4. Amber Hunt and David Batcher. *The Kennedy Wives: Triumph and Tragedy in America's Most Public Family.* Guilford, CT: Lyons, 2014. Print. 178.

5. "Jacqueline Kennedy in the White House." *John F. Kennedy Presidential Library and Museum.* John F. Kennedy Presidential Library and Museum, n.d. Web. 5 Aug. 2015.

6. "The Cold War." *John F. Kennedy Presidential Library and Museum.* John F. Kennedy Presidential Library and Museum, n.d. Web. 5 Aug. 2015.

7. "Milestones: 1953–1960." *US Department of State Office of the Historian.* Office of the Historian, n.d. Web. 5 Aug. 2015.

8. "Berlin Wall." *History.* A&E Television Networks, 2015. Web. 5 Aug. 2015.

9. "The Presidents: The Kennedys." *American Experience.* PBS. WGBH, Boston. 2008. Television.

10. "John F. Kennedy: Domestic Affairs." *Miller Center.* Rector and Visitors of University of Virginia, n.d. Web. 5 Aug. 2015.

11. "Cuban Missile Crisis Address to the Nation." *American Rhetoric*. American Rhetoric, 2015. Web. 16 Oct. 2015.

12. "Nuclear Test Ban Treaty." *John F. Kennedy Presidential Library and Museum*. John F. Kennedy Presidential Library and Museum, n.d. Web. 5 Aug. 2015.

13. "Document for September 22nd: Executive Order 10924: Establishment of the Peace Corps." *National Archives*. US National Archives and Record Administration, 1 Mar. 1961. Web. 5 Aug. 2015.

14. Henry Louis Gates Jr. "How Black Was JFK's Camelot?" *Root*. Slate Group, 18 Nov. 2013. Web. 5 Aug. 2015.

15. "Primary Resources: JFK on Civil Rights." *American Experience*. WGBH, 2013. Web. 5 Aug. 2015.

16. "How NASA's Space Race Helped to Integrate the South." *NPR*. NPR, 6 May 2015. Web. 5 Aug. 2015.

CHAPTER 6. JOHN F. KENNEDY ASSASSINATED

1. Jesse Greenspan. "The Other Victims of the JFK Assassination." *History*. A&E Television Networks, 18 Nov. 2013. Web. 5 Aug. 2015.

2. Michael Meagher and Larry D. Gragg. *John F. Kennedy: A Biography*. Santa Barbara, CA: Greenwood, 2011. Print. 129.

3. Tom Wicker. "Kennedy Is Killed by Sniper as He Rides in Car in Dallas; Johnson Sworn In on Plane." *New York Times*. New York Times Company, 22 Nov. 1963. Web. 5 Aug. 2015.

4. Ibid.

5. "Warren Commission Hearings: Vol. XIV–page 561." *John F. Kennedy Assassination Homepage*. jfk-assassination.com, 5 Dec. 2004. Web. 5 Aug. 2015.

6. "Conspiracy Theories: The JFK Assassination." *Time*. Time, 2015. Web. 5 Aug. 2015.

7. "JFK's Funeral: Photos from a Day of Shock and Grief." *LIFE*. Time, 2014. Web. 5 Aug. 2015.

8. Larry McShane. "The Day America Watched a Son's Final Salute to Slain Father, JFK, as Nation Buried a Beloved Leader." *Daily News*. NYDailyNews.com, 17 Nov. 2013. Web. 5 Aug. 2015.

9. "'The Picture of the Funeral': JFK Jr. Salutes His Father's Casket." *UPI*. United Press International, 25 Nov. 2013. Web. 5 Aug. 2015.

CHAPTER 7. BOBBY TAKES THE REINS

1. "JFK on the Economy and Taxes." *John F. Kennedy Presidential Library and Museum*. John F. Kennedy Presidential Library and Museum, n.d. Web. 5 Aug. 2015.

2. "Robert F. Kennedy." *John F. Kennedy Presidential Library and Museum*. John F. Kennedy Presidential Library and Museum, n.d. Web. 5 Aug. 2015.

3. Jack Newfield. "Robert Kennedy: A Memoir." *Kennedys: Stories of Life and Death from an American Family*. Ed. Clint Willis. New York: Thunder's Mouth, 2001. Print. 209.

4. "Robert F. Kennedy." *John F. Kennedy Presidential Library and Museum*. John F. Kennedy Presidential Library and Museum, n.d. Web. 5 Aug. 2015.

5. "Selected Quotes." *Robert F. Kennedy Center for Justice & Human Rights*. Robert F. Kennedy Center for Justice & Human Rights, 2015. Web. 5 Aug. 2015.

6. Ronald Steel. "In Love with Night." *Kennedys: Stories of Life and Death from an American Family.* Ed. Clint Willis. New York: Thunder's Mouth, 2001. Print. 223.

7. Jake Mooney. "Star Power, Still Shining 40 Years On." *New York Times.* New York Times Company, 29 Jan. 2009. Web. 5 Aug. 2015.

8. "US Army Campaigns: Vietnam." *Center of Military History.* US Army Center of Military History, 13 July 2015. Web. 5 Aug. 2015.

9. "Robert F. Kennedy." *Robert F. Kennedy Center for Justice & Human Rights.* Robert F. Kennedy Center for Justice & Human Rights, 2015. Web. 5 Aug. 2015.

10. Ronald Steel. "In Love with Night." *Kennedys: Stories of Life and Death from an American Family.* Ed. Clint Willis. New York: Thunder's Mouth, 2001. Print. 220.

11. Ibid. 221.

CHAPTER 8. TED'S CAREER IN THE SENATE

1. Ned Potter. "Edward M. Kennedy Escaped Death in 1964." *ABC News.* ABC News, 27 Aug. 2009. Web. 5 Aug. 2015.

2. "The Presidents: The Kennedys." *American Experience.* PBS. WGBH, Boston. 2008. Television.

3. Ibid.

4. "Ted Kennedy Car Accident in Chappaquiddick." *Newsweek.* Newsweek, 3 Aug. 1969. Web. 5 Aug. 2015.

5. "The Presidents: The Kennedys." *American Experience.* PBS. WGBH, Boston. 2008. Television.

6. Ibid.

7. "Seventh Term: 1995–2000." *Edward M. Kennedy Institute for the United States Senate.* Edward M. Kennedy Institute for the United States Senate, 2015. Web. 5 Aug. 2015.

8. "Children's Health Insurance Program Overview." *National Conference of State Legislatures.* National Conference of State Legislatures, 17 Apr. 2015. Web. 5 Aug. 2015.

9. John M. Broder. "Social Causes Defined Kennedy, Even at the End of a 46-Year Career in the Senate." *New York Times.* New York Times Company, 26 Aug. 2009. Web. 5 Aug. 2015.

10. Vincent Bzdek. *The Kennedy Legacy: Jack, Bobby and Ted and a Family Dream Fulfilled.* New York: Palgrave Macmillan, 2009. Print. 9.

11. John M. Broder. "Social Causes Defined Kennedy, Even at the End of a 46-Year Career in the Senate." *New York Times.* New York Times Company, 26 Aug. 2009. Web. 5 Aug. 2015.

12. "Ninth Term: 2007–2009." *Edward M. Kennedy Institute for the United States Senate.* Edward M. Kennedy Institute for the United States Senate, 2015. Web. 5 Aug. 2015.

CHAPTER 9. THE KENNEDY LEGACY

1. Jill Lawrence. "The Kennedy Family Legacy." *ABC News.* ABC News, 2015. Web. 5 Aug. 2015.

2. Arthur M. Schlesinger. *Robert Kennedy and His Times.* Boston: Houghton, 2002. Print. 787–790.

3. Jill Lawrence. "The Kennedy Family Legacy." *ABC News.* ABC News, 2015. Web. 5 Aug. 2015.

Alexis Burling has written dozens of articles and books for young readers on a variety of topics including current events and famous people, nutrition and fitness, careers and money management, relationships, and cooking. She is also a book critic (and an obsessive reader!). Her reviews of both adult and young adult books, author interviews, and other publishing industry–related articles have appeared in the *New York Times*, the *Washington Post*, the *Chicago Tribune*, and more.